CONFRONTING CAPITALISM

CONFRONTING
CAPITALISM

REAL SOLUTIONS
FOR A TROUBLED ECONOMIC SYSTEM

PHILIP KOTLER

AMACOM
AMERICAN MANAGEMENT ASSOCIATION
NEW YORK • ATLANTA • BRUSSELS • CHICAGO • MEXICO CITY
SAN FRANCISCO • SHANGHAI • TOKYO • TORONTO • WASHINGTON, D.C.

Bulk discounts available. For details visit: www.amacombooks.org/go/specialsales
Or contact special sales: Phone: 800-250-5308 Email: specialsls@amanet.org
View all the AMACOM titles at: www.amacombooks.org
American Management Association: www.amanet.org

This publication is designed to provide accurate and authoritative information in regard to the subject matter covered. It is sold with the understanding that the publisher is not engaged in rendering legal, accounting, or other professional service. If legal advice or other expert assistance is required, the services of a competent professional person should be sought.

LIBRARY OF CONGRESS CATALOGING-IN-PUBLICATION DATA
Kotler, Philip.
Confronting capitalism : real solutions for a troubled economic system /
Philip Kotler. -- 1 Edition.
pages cm
Includes index.
ISBN 978-0-8144-3645-5 (hardcover) -- ISBN 0-8144-3645-5 (hardcover) --
ISBN 978-0-8144-3646-2 (e-book) 1. Capitalism. 2. Capitalism--Social aspects.
3. Economic policy. I. Title.
HB501.K5966 2015
330.12'2--dc23   2014042242

About AMA

American Management Association (www.amanet.org) is a world leader in talent development, advancing the skills of individuals to drive business success. Our mission is to support the goals of individuals and organizations through a complete range of products and services, including classroom and virtual seminars, webcasts, webinars, podcasts, conferences, corporate and government solutions, business books, and research. AMA's approach to improving performance combines experiential learning—learning through doing—with opportunities for ongoing professional growth at every step of one's career journey.

Printing number
10 9 8 7 6 5 4 3 2 1

CONTENTS

CONFRONTING CAPITALISM

CREATING HIGH-PERFORMANCE CAPITALISM

The difference between what we are doing and what we are capable of doing would solve most of the world's problems.

—MAHATMA GANDHI

There are scores of books on capitalism, most of them defending it, several criticizing it, and many just trying to explain it. Why would anyone want to write another book on capitalism?

I have five reasons for doing so.

First, I want to understand it myself. My family, friends, and acquaintances around the world live in a market economy run on a system called capitalism. They tell me they want to understand capitalism better.

Second, I believe capitalism is better than any other system. But I also believe that it has *fourteen major shortcomings*. I wanted to examine these shortcomings and their ramifications.

Third, I want to examine and propose solutions to each of the fourteen shortcomings that would help make capitalism perform better and benefit more people.

Fourth, many readers want a shorter book on capitalism to get their thinking started. Thomas Piketty's book, *Capital in the Twenty-First Century* (Belknap Press, 2014), has sold over 200,000 copies, but most book buyers did not read the 500 or so pages beyond the first couple of chapters. In this busy age, we need more concise accounts of social and economic systems that deeply affect our lives. Piketty focused only on income inequality, which is only one of fourteen shortcomings of capitalism that need to be examined.

Fifth, I believe that my background provides an opportunity to develop some special insights into the workings of capitalism. I am a classically trained economist who studied under three great and opposite-thinking Nobel Prize–winning economists, namely, Professor Milton Friedman of the University of Chicago, who represented free market thinking, and Professors Paul Samuelson and Robert Solow of MIT, who represented Keynesian thinking. My goal was to apply macro- and microeconomic theory to understand company decision making aimed at winning market share in highly competitive markets. I feel that economists have neglected the role and power of marketing to shape and influence markets. Marketing is one of the bedrock concepts in a capitalist society. As a behaviorally oriented market economist, I focus my attention on the functioning of the five major players in a market economy: business enterprises, nonprofit organizations, financiers, households, and government. Capitalism, management, and marketing must be joined into a comprehensive framework to understand marketplace developments and impacts. I hope this book achieves that goal.

You'll read in today's media about other ideas proposing improved forms of capitalism, including Compassionate Capitalism, Inclusive Capitalism, Humane Capitalism, Humanistic Capitalism, Healthy Capitalism, and Neo-Capitalism. These are all efforts to improve both the image and the functioning of capitalism. There is a broad swath of public opinion suggesting that people want to end "Cowboy Capitalism"— where anything and everything is acceptable in the pursuit of profits.

They want to save capitalism from itself as it continues to disenfranchise and disenchant many citizens.

In 2014, the Harvard Business School surveyed its alumni and reported this finding: "The United States is competitive to the extent that firms operating here do two things: win in global markets and lift the living standards of average Americans. The U.S. economy is doing the first of these but failing at the second." Recently, Harvard professor Michael Porter went on to say: "This is a critical moment for our nation. Business leaders and policy makers need a strategy to get our country on a path towards broadly shared prosperity." Professor Jan Rivkin added, "Firms can escape the weaknesses in the U.S. business environment by moving abroad, but workers can't."[1]

Capitalism is still morphing. Today we are living in an era of globalized capitalism. While it has improved since the era of the 1900s when exceedingly harsh working conditions were the norm, we still have sweatshops and migrant workers living on starvation wages in many parts of the world today. Capitalism has been improving, but there is some distance to go.

People tend to think of capitalism as consisting of large corporate multinationals and financial organizations. Some have called this Corporate Capitalism. But we should not forget that one-man firms, mom-and-pop stores, and small businesses with five to ten workers account for a great number of enterprises in developed economies. (In less developed economies, they account for up to 90 percent of the economy.) We hope they can adopt modern business practices and improve their productivity and performance and grow their businesses.

Most countries have chosen capitalistic concepts to run all or part of their market economy. The market economy is divided into five specific markets: (1) businesses, (2) nonprofits, (3) financiers, (4) government, and (5) households. Countries differ in how they treat these five markets. China doesn't have a free financial market, but it does have a private business market. The United States has a large government market, while Ireland has a small government market. The U.S. has a very large household credit market; many countries don't. The U.S. also has a large nonprofit organization market; most countries don't.

Some countries prefer to describe their market economy as socialistic rather than capitalistic. For example, India designates its system as socialist, not capitalist. China calls its system socialism, but it's really a market economy with Chinese characteristics. Sweden formerly said it operates a "mixed economy," but now calls it a "welfare economy."

The term "welfare economy" suggests that the market economy tries to balance private enterprise with social purpose. The Nordic countries are a prime example. They want their business enterprises to pay living wages and provide good working conditions for their employees and their families. They put a high premium on education and health for all. Their companies provide long vacation time and generous time off for working mothers who give birth. They cannot fire workers without cause and must compensate those who have been dismissed. These market economies have been called "capitalism with a conscience" or "capitalism with a heart."

Britain's Labour Party also takes a "public welfare" point of view. Its new leader, Ed Miliband, recommended the following policies at Labour's annual conference in September 2014: Increasing the minimum wage and reverting the income tax of the highest earners back to 50 percent as well as "a new tax on 'mansions'; a freeze on electricity prices; special taxes on hedge funds and tobacco companies; further taxes on bankers' bonuses; and yet another increase in the levy that banks pay according to the size of their balance sheet."[2] This supplies a picture of the reform measures that "free market" critics want to introduce to improve the conditions of average workers.

Strict socialist economies tend to go further in controlling the business of the economy. The leaders of Cuba, Venezuela, Bolivia, and Ecuador prefer state-operated businesses and tend to be anticapitalist. They dismiss the profit motive and claim that the state is able to run businesses efficiently. They focus on raising the living standards of the poor. They spend effort on developing a good education and health system. Too often, however, they lose the support of those inside and outside of the country who have capital to invest. This limits their ability to grow their gross domestic product, and the danger is that their anticapitalist stand will make more of their people poorer. Politically, they prefer to import from those countries that have the same ideology, and their citizens don't end up with much product choice. Critics see these countries as having less competition, less freedom, and less consumer choice.

Citizens of a country face a choice between three types of economic systems. At one extreme is "unregulated capitalism." In the middle is "capitalism with a heart." At the other extreme is "strict socialism." My own choice, dear reader, lies in the middle.

In different countries, citizens will vary in their ability to start and own their own businesses. The degree of ease in starting a business, growing it, and handling regulations and licenses will differ from country to country. Many countries never realize the full power of capitalism to improve the lives of their citizens because they require too much licensing or regulation, not to mention widespread corruption or criminality in some cases. Clearly, we need to moderate taxes and burdens on capitalism so that capitalism will be allowed to work its wonders.

THE SUCCESSES OF CAPITALISM

Today capitalism rules supreme. But capitalism was at war with another system, communism, for over seventy years, from 1917 to 1989. On November 9, 1989, the Berlin Wall started to come down. Symbolically, this event represented the crumbling of the Union of Soviet Socialist Republics (USSR). The Soviet Union's economy was wholly state-owned and state-controlled. The economy in the USSR operated on a succession of five-year plans, spelling out how much food, steel, consumer goods, capital goods, highways, electrical grids, waste treatment systems, and other items of material value would be produced. It was a command-and-control economy.

The Soviet Union was supposed to produce a worker's paradise. Instead, Soviet citizens faced long lines and frequent shortages of bread, meat, and potatoes. Their washing machines, radios, and television sets were of poor quality, very little innovation occurred, and worker productivity was pathetically low. As Soviet workers assessed their situation: "They pretend to pay us. We pretend to work."

What's more, communism took on the markings of a tyranny with little freedom of speech, no independent newspapers, and dissidents sent to jail. The USSR's major newspaper was called *Pravda*, which means "Truth" in Russian—an ironic national joke and disgrace. The number of people killed under the regime of Joseph Stalin, the dictator who ruled the Soviet Union from 1922 until his death in 1953, has been estimated at between 20 million and 60 million by some scholars and historians.[3]

Soviet communism finally crumbled and the Soviet Union disintegrated into several independent countries, leaving Russia to determine its own fate. Each of these new countries needed to develop its own version of an economic system, relying mostly on its past communist heritage.

China, too, began as a communist regime under Chairman Mao Zedong with the creation of the People's Republic in 1949. Its worst tyrannical period was during the Cultural Revolution, starting in 1966 and running ten years until the death of Mao in 1976. Economic reforms were finally introduced in 1978. Now China is one of the world's fastest-growing major economies. By October 2014, China became the world's largest economy and the world's largest exporter and importer of goods. China has become the world's factory. More Chinese people were moved out of poverty in a shorter time period than ever before. Today China reports that it has 350 million people who are millionaires, which would amount to a numerically larger middle class than found in the United

States. The irony is that China still views itself as running a communist system, but its miracle performance occurred after it adopted what can be called "authoritarian capitalism."

The common opinion is that virtually all nations now run a capitalist-oriented market economy. Laissez-faire capitalists, such as Milton Friedman and Allan Meltzer, would argue, "Capitalism has won. Capitalism has been a success story in improving the lives of people. Capitalism has delivered more *growth* and *freedom* than any other system."[4] But we need to understand that there are many different national versions of capitalist theory and practice.

WHAT IS CAPITALISM?

Capitalism assumes a constitutional legal system based on three fundamental concepts: *private property*, *contracts*, and *the rule of law*. People have the right to own private property. People are free to enter contracts with others over the use of products, services, and property. Contracts are honored and governed by the rule of law. Note that every country, even tyrannies, claim to have a legal system. But in many cases, the system is riddled with privilege, politics, corruption, and inefficiency.

Capitalism assumes that there is a constitutional government with legislative, executive, and judicial powers and the force to carry out the rule of law. The sovereign power can enforce laws and back them with penal power.

Capitalism also begins with the idea that some members of the society own capital in the form of money, property, equipment, and goods. These capital owners are free to start any business. They can ask for loans from banks or others who believe in their business idea. Some of these new businesses will grow and create new jobs. Others will flounder. But the basic idea is that there is freedom to start and to operate a business. Owners are free to promote their products and seek customers. If they attract enough customers who are satisfied and who recommend their goods and services to other customers, they are on their way to growth and profits.

When business creators face relatively few encumbrances, we call it free market capitalism. This is a largely self-regulating system without excessive regulation or government subsidies. Businesses succeed if they can attract, keep, and grow customers. The customers decide which businesses succeed. Much depends on the ability of a business to know its customers well, to monitor their changing needs and expectations, and to generate continuous and new value for its customers.

As companies grow bigger, they usually benefit from *economies of scale*: Their unit costs fall because their fixed costs are spread over more units of production. With lower costs than smaller competitors, and a stronger brand name, they can increase their market share. Often they grow by buying smaller competitors who lack scale. They can also grow by exploiting *economies of scope*, namely, by expanding the number of items and product categories they handle. If a consumer packaged-goods company sells its product to supermarkets, it would benefit from selling additional products to the same supermarkets. This way it gains economies of scope because of lower transaction costs per product with supermarkets. Thus Procter & Gamble, which sells over a hundred different products to supermarkets, has a distinct power advantage over companies that sell only one product to supermarkets.

The combination of economies of scale and scope has led to the growth of giant multinational firms. The 200 largest industrial corporations—multinationals such as Wal-Mart, Royal Dutch Shell, Toyota, and Samsung Electronics—account for 28 percent of the world's gross domestic product (GDP).[5] Several industries operate as oligopolies, where a few large firms account for the major market share in a product category. Thus, there are a limited number of large aircraft manufacturers—Boeing and Airbus (actually a duopoly)—and a limited number of large airlines in a nation—United, American, and Delta in the United States. The U.S. remains a nation with a huge number of small businesses ($0 to $10 million revenue or employing fewer than fifty people) and 197,000 medium-size businesses ($10 million to $1 billion annual revenue), but it also has oligopolies that generate a good percentage of their revenue from overseas, maybe approaching a 50 percent share of the U.S. GDP.

The U.S. economy is increasingly run by a "visible hand" instead of Adam Smith's "invisible hand." Large sectors of the economy are guided by a few powerful companies. The question is whether the visible hand runs these sectors with Smith's "enlightened self-interest" or with just "self-interest." (The issue of social justice will be examined later.)

In our market economy, companies know their competitors. If they aren't the leader in their industry, they aspire either to follow the leader or compete with the leader in search of more profit and growth. Competition today is hypercompetitive. During a recession many businesses go under, with their assets often bought by surviving competitors. The intense competition keeps prices low (in the absence of collusive activity) and keeps quality and innovation high—three highly desirable traits of a capitalistic economy. The entrance of foreign competitors with still lower costs also keeps domestic companies on continuous alert lest they should be overwhelmed and lose their domestic customers.

In the best cases, capitalism is powered by individualism, ambition, a competitive spirit, collaboration, and good management systems.

Capitalism is a system in which businesses search for latent or unsatisfied needs that they can satisfy and make a profit by satisfying. Profit is the reward for creating satisfied customers. Successful businesses can use the profit as pay to the owners and investors, or pay more to the other stakeholders, or retain the profit to grow their business bigger.

The major issue regarding capitalism is: How free should it be from government regulation and spending? At one extreme are those who hold that government should be minimal in its interventions and regulations (laissez-faire). This is the position articulated by Friedrich Hayek and Milton Friedman, whose writings influenced Ronald Reagan and

Margaret Thatcher to push forth the neoliberalist position, much in line with classical economics of minimal government, low tax rates, deregulation, free trade, open markets, and privatization.

At the other extreme is the welfare view, which holds that government should play an active regulatory role, a social welfare role, and an intervention role in times of economic distress. On this issue of the role of government, capitalist countries differ from one extreme to the other, with everything in between.

CRITICS OF CAPITALISM

Capitalism has its share of eminent critics. The famous British economist John Maynard Keynes wondered whether capitalism could ever benefit everyone. He said: "Capitalism is the extraordinary belief that the nastiest of men for the nastiest of motives will somehow work for the benefit of all." Meanwhile, the great British leader Winston Churchill saw capitalism as better than socialism. His assessment: "The inherent vice of capitalism is the unequal sharing of blessings; the inherent virtue of socialism is the equal sharing of miseries."

Proponents of capitalism often act as if it is the Shining City on the Hill that all other people should look up to and admire, but capitalism has plenty of shortcomings. In spite of the accomplishments of capitalism in raising the standard of living of so many people around the world, critics will point to specific problems, such as companies failing to pay living wages, not covering full social costs, neglecting the environment, and overpaying a few at the expense of the many.

Other critics specifically target laissez-faire or crony capitalism. Jerry Mander, author of *The Capitalism Papers: Fatal Flaws of an Obsolete System* (Counterpoint, 2013), sees capitalism as destroying our environment, our communities, our well-being, and our very humanity. Naomi Klein, in her book *The Shock Doctrine: The Rise of Disaster Capitalism* (Picador, 2008), sees laissez-faire or Cowboy Capitalism as destroying the middle class; making the rich richer and the poor poorer; reducing economic growth; eliminating the union movement; introducing privatization, deregulation, and cutbacks in social welfare spending; giving special favors to large multinationals; and creating a form of capitalism marked by instability and frequent booms and busts. She sees capitalism as run by a government/business/finance/military complex designed to withhold help from the workers and the poor.

In examining capitalism's entry into different countries such as Chile, Argentina, Russia, Poland, and others, Klein documents what privatization is doing. Because city, state, and national governments are cash poor, they are selling normal government functions to private firms. Many American communities have privatized garbage collection, water treatment, and parking meter tax collection. Schools and hospitals are being privatized. Klein describes how privatization has led to higher food prices, an exponential rise in the number of destitute persons, and a decline in human rights. She claims that privatization often is accompanied by using fewer workers or paying lower wages, rather than increasing efficiency in other ways. She labels all of this "disaster capitalism." She and other critics point to the United States having the world's highest divorce rate, very high maternal and infant mortality rates, an extremely high rate of childhood poverty, the highest rate of adult obesity, the highest prison incarceration rate, and the second-highest murder rate.

In *Das Capital*, Karl Marx was unrelenting in his criticism of capitalism. He postulated that capitalism exploited the working class and dispossessed them of any property. He saw the workers as wage-slaves without any chance to improve their condition. To Marx, the capitalist economy consisted of two classes: those who owned property and the proletarians who didn't. Those who owned property would hire those without property, pay them as little as possible, and keep them in a state of virtual slavery, working long hours and seven days a week in some cases. The reserve army of the unemployed assured continuous pressure for low wages. The anticapitalist rhetoric that arose from Marx and Friedrich Engels's writings lasts to this day in some critics' minds.

Much has improved in modern capitalism. Consider how contemporary business management practices have improved efficiency and productivity. Consider the many technologies that innovation-driven capitalism has created for better living. Consider the rise of legislation and regulations to reduce or correct potential consumer and business abuses.

Yet a book with the intriguing title *How Much Have Global Problems Cost the World?*[6] examines and estimates the actual costs, between 1900 and 2050, from such problems as air pollution, armed conflict, climate change, ecosystems/biodiversity, education, gender inequality, human health, malnutrition, trade barriers, and water/sanitation. Capitalism is not to blame for all of these problems. Although the estimates can be questioned, the point is well made that these problems have imposed a very high cost, almost always exceeding the cost of remedying or removing them.

THE FOURTEEN SHORTCOMINGS OF CAPITALISM

Here are what I consider to be the fourteen serious shortcomings of capitalism that need to be addressed and remedied to whatever extent possible. I believe that capitalism:

1. Proposes little or no solution to persisting poverty
2. Generates a growing level of income and wealth inequality
3. Fails to pay a living wage to billions of workers
4. May not provide enough human jobs in the face of growing automation
5. Doesn't charge businesses with the full social costs of their activities

6. Exploits the environment and natural resources in the absence of regulation

7. Creates business cycles and economic instability

8. Emphasizes individualism and self-interest at the expense of community and the commons

9. Encourages high consumer debt and leads to a growing financially driven rather than producer-driven economy

10. Lets politicians and business interests collaborate to subvert the economic interests of the majority of citizens

11. Favors short-run profit planning over long-run investment planning

12. Should have regulations regarding product quality, safety, truth in advertising, and anticompetitive behavior

13. Tends to focus narrowly on GDP growth

14. Needs to bring social values and happiness into the market equation

My aim is to examine each of these shortcomings and the underlying forces and causes and propose possible solutions. Hopefully, capitalism can do a better job of reducing poverty. Hopefully, capitalism can constrain income disparity from growing more severe. Hopefully, capitalism can be more careful and caring in its impact on the environment. And so on.

This book discusses how capitalism plays out in the United States as well as in many other countries of the world. As more countries move to a higher level of economic development, their problems will resemble more closely the problems, and the solutions, that play out in the United States. It is important that the citizens in each country examine the same questions and shortcomings about capitalism in their country. What role does capitalism play? How does the form of capitalism in their country relate to the form of democracy in their country? What are the major shortcomings of capitalism in their country? What are the available tools and solutions that will improve the performance of capitalism in their country?

The great composer Igor Stravinsky once said, "There is no problem without a solution." If an individual or group wants something strongly enough, then the very existence of the problem guarantees that a solution also exists somewhere. We persisted and ended slavery, we established women's voting rights and their right to make decisions involving their own bodies, we legislated gay rights, and so on. Victor Hugo put it so well: "There is one thing stronger than all the armies in the world, and that is an idea whose time has come."

I'm not looking for an alternative to capitalism. Remember Winston Churchill's famous defense of democracy: "Democracy is the worst form of government, except for all those other forms that have been tried from time to time."[7] I accept the possibility that capitalism may be a poor way to run an economy, except for all the other forms that have been tried and failed.

At the same time, it's true that the capitalism that grew out of the West is beset with problems. The West is losing its relative power and influence in the world and is saddled with slow economic growth, high unemployment, huge government deficits, heavy public debt, low savings rates, a declining work ethic, and rampant drugs and crime.

I don't believe, as some do, that a further decline in the West is inevitable. I remain optimistic about the world's countries improving the lives of their people. There are many business and other groups at work trying to create a stronger capitalism that serves consumers, workers, and citizens better and improves the environment rather than destroys or neglects it.

As one example, consider the capitalist reform movement called Conscious Capitalism (www.consciouscapitalism.com), which includes the CEOs of companies such as Whole Foods, Panera Bread, The Container Company, and others. It has four tenets:

1. Companies should embrace a *higher purpose* for their business than just profits.
2. Companies should seek to benefit not only the investors but all the involved *stakeholders* in shared prosperity.
3. Company leaders need to be committed to the *community respon-sibilities* of their company.
4. The company's *culture* should place a strong value on trust, authenticity, caring, transparency, integrity, learning, and empowerment.

Another movement is called the New Economy Movement. Its aim is to place more business and capital in the hands of the 99 percent rather than the one percent. It offers a different model, worker-owned-and-managed enterprises, than Corporate Capitalism. Gar Alperovitz, one of its leaders, describes the range of organizations under cooperative ownership and operation:

> More than 130 million Americans, in fact, already belong to one or another form of cooperative—and especially the most widely known form: the credit union. Similarly, there are some 2,000 municipally owned utilities, a number of which are ecological leaders . . . Upwards of 10 million Americans now also work at some 11,000 employee-owned firms (ESOP companies).[8]

Movements such as the New Economy and Conscious Capitalism are designing new models of capitalism that aim to create more citizen ownership and participation and more stakeholder benefits. They are searching for a more enlightened and constructive capitalism.

Let's now move to consider the fourteen shortcomings of capitalism, one described in each of the following chapters, and their potential solutions.

ONE

THE PERSISTENCE OF POVERTY

No society can surely be flourishing and happy, of which the far greater part of the members are poor and miserable.

— ADAM SMITH, *The Wealth of Nations*

Poverty is one of the most intractable and shameful problems mankind has had to deal with. Today, about 5 billion of the 7 billion people inhabiting the earth are poor or extremely poor. They go hungry. They have no energy or time for education. They are susceptible to disease because of little or no access to health care. They often have more children than they can support, which perpetuates a poverty class, a culture of poverty. Their hopeless condition leads some of the poor into lives of crime, hard drugs, and armed conflict. This means that the cost of poverty far exceeds the cost that the poor themselves bear. Poverty pours its poison on the rest of mankind.

Until the nineteenth century, the poor received little attention. Poverty was seen to be inevitable. Governments and do-gooders could do little about it. The Industrial Revolution exacerbated the problem in attracting poor rural peasants to the cities in search of work, leading to the establishment of shantytowns and poorhouses. The four worst slums in the world today are Dharavi in Mumbai, Orangi in Pakistan, Kibera in Nairobi, and the Favelas in Rio de Janeiro.

The plight of the poor became more visible in the nineteenth century with the publication in 1838 of *Oliver Twist* by Charles Dickens. *Oliver Twist* vividly dramatized the conditions and exploitation of the poor. Around the turn of the century, careful and caring researchers, such as Beatrice and Sidney Webb in the United Kingdom, started to count the number of poor and write about their plight.

The concept of creating antipoverty programs began in the nineteenth century and continues through today, when one-sixth of the world's population earns less than $1 a day. (Another 2 billion of the world's 7 billion people earn less than $2 a day.) U.S. president Lyndon Johnson declared an "unconditional war" on poverty in the mid-1960s. He helped pass enlightened legislation to reduce the level of U.S. poverty, including Medicaid, unemployment insurance, Head Start, and many other programs. In 1975, the "earned income tax credit" was enacted, which refunds to the working poor some of their income and payroll taxes. The EITC has averaged about $3,000 for families with one child and up to $6,000 for those with three or more children.

Finally, in the year 2000, the United Nations outlined its multilateral plan for reducing world poverty. The United Nations formulated the Millennium Development Goals (MDG), specifically eight goals with eighteen accompanying targets, designed to significantly reduce poverty levels by 2015. Target 1 was to cut in half, between 1990 and 2015, the proportion of people whose income is less than one dollar a day. Other goals include achieving universal primary education; promoting gender equality; reducing child mortality; improving maternal health; combating HIV/AIDS, malaria, and other diseases; ensuring environmental sustainability; and forming a global partnership in development. The goals are ambitious and all are not likely to be achieved, given the Great Recession starting in 2008, rising food and energy costs, and continued armed conflict in the world. World leaders are now asking the United Nations headquarters to take bolder action against extreme poverty, hunger, and disease and to adopt in 2015 the next set of antipoverty goals.

THE CAUSES OF POVERTY

Experts have put forth several different theories on the causes of poverty and advocated different measures to cure the problem. We can distinguish between experts who see poverty as having one major basic cause and those who see many causal factors at work.

The simplest theory is that the poor have brought the condition on themselves. Many who are poor did not care to learn anything in school, dropped out early, took on work requiring no skill, spent some of their income on drink, drugs, and gambling, got married too early, and had more children than they could support. Their children carried on the same indifference to education and skill building. Often the marriage broke up. Some who lost their job preferred to live on transfer payments like Medicaid, housing subsidies, food stamps, or disability payments rather than take on low-paid work. The solution is either to find ways to change their attitudes and behavior or leave them in their penurious state. Yet there is ample evidence that most of the poor would be ready and willing to escape their impoverished conditions if they could find employment and have a decent place to live.

Another theory is that poverty is the result of the poor having too many children. Each new child makes a poor family poorer. The argument goes further to say that the earth has a limited population "carrying capacity" for resources and food to permit a decent standard of living for 7 billion people, let alone the 9 billion people projected for 2050.[1] Soil erosion over the past forty years has rendered 30 percent of the world's arable land unproductive. Agriculture today uses 70 percent of the world's freshwater. The heat and drought caused by climate warming reduce crop yields by 2 percent every ten years. So the problem is how to grow more food on less farmland with less water.

Under this theory, poverty continues to be a problem because of overpopulation. This is a version of Thomas Malthus's eighteenth-century proposition that the rate of population growth sooner or later will exceed the rate of growth of food supply, resulting in starvation, war, and the continuation of poverty.[2] The modern version of this view was published in 1972 in *The Limits to Growth* by Donella H. and Dennis L. Meadows (with Jørgen Randers and William W. Behrens III).[3] Here the solution follows that much poverty would abate if poor families would limit the number of their offspring voluntarily or by edict. China represents the latter in generally restricting families to bearing only one child. While the "one-child" policy now has several exceptions, it is estimated that between 1979 and 2009, approximately 200 million births were averted in China. Certainly this has been one of the major contributors to China's impressive reduction in the number of families living in poverty.

A third theory is that poverty persists because the poor don't own any fungible property or capital on which they could borrow money. They lack tradable assets. This theory has been propounded by the highly respected, though controversial, Peruvian economist Hernando de Soto in his book *The Mystery of Capital: Why Capitalism Triumphs in the West and Fails Everywhere Else* (Basic Books, 2010). De Soto argues that the actual source of wealth is real property, along with the existence of well-defined and socially accepted property rights. Property is an asset that can be used to get a loan or mortgage or obtain insurance or own stock and other things that make capitalism so effective in producing economic growth and prosperity. But, de Soto says, capitalism doesn't work in poor communities and countries because the financial institutions don't recognize the assets of the poor.

The poor have plenty of assets (land, homes, businesses), but these lie typically in the extralegal, informal realm. The legal system has not adapted to this reality. The costs of making these assets legal (obtaining proper title to a house, registering a business, etc.) are so prohibitive in terms of time and money that the assets end up being "dead capital." The poor cannot use their assets for credit to acquire the normal capitalist tools to achieve upward mobility. Because these assets are not recognized, they create an extralegal style of living within their informal social circles. For Hernando de Soto, the singular solution is to push the legal system to allow the monetization of these assets so the dead capital becomes alive.

Still another theory blames poverty on the greed of the ruling elite. The theory starts by drawing a distinction between *economic growth* and *economic development.* You can have economic growth without economic development. Economic growth is a necessary but not sufficient condition of economic development. Economic growth simply means that the pie (measured by GDP) has grown bigger, but it says nothing about how the pie is divided.

Economic development differs in being concerned with whether the average person's standard of living has increased and whether the person has more freedom of choice. Economic development can be measured by the Human Development Index. The HDI takes into account literacy rates, gender parity, and life expectancy, which affect productivity and could lead to economic growth. Economic development implies an increase in real income for most families. Economic development seeks to alleviate people from low standards of living and works toward providing citizens with jobs and suitable shelter. It seeks to improve lives without compromising the needs of future generations. On the other hand, economic growth does not address the question of the depletion of natural resources and pollution and global warming.

The difference between economic growth and economic development is well illustrated by the African country of Angola, where the GDP grew by 20 percent and yet poverty increased substantially. Much of the higher GDP flowed into the pockets of the ruling elites and their relatives and cronies. The daughter of the president of Angola herself was a billionaire and yet did nothing to create value for Angola. By contrast, Bill Gates built a business called Microsoft that made him a billionaire many times over, but at least the business contributed to the development of the U.S. economy and jobs.

Egypt's past ruler, Hosni Mubarak, had a fortune estimated at $42 billion. Many ministers in African countries are billionaires. Where did this money come from? A great deal came from foreign aid designed to help with economic development, most of which ended up in the pockets of the ruling elite.

Most African countries claim that Africa's deep and persistent poverty is due to the years of Western colonialism and imperialism. This is more an excuse that African dictators propagate to stay in power. The real cause of African poverty is bad African governance following independence, not colonialism. African countries made two mistakes after achieving independence. First, most African countries established a one-party state system with a president for life. This alone caused much of the wealth to flow to the president's extended family and cronies and led most other groups to be excluded from both governing and sharing in the benefits.

Second, most African countries established a socialist rather than a capitalist economic system with many state-owned enterprises (SOEs) to run the utilities, produce the steel and oil and other basic products, and carry on the commerce and trade of the nation. By contrast, South Korea emerged after the Second World War as a poor country comparable to African economies, but went capitalistic and today stands as a wealthy country with high citizen incomes and participation.

Why do civil wars plague the African continent? Because many of the countries are headed by a dictator whose family takes most of the "goodies." Some groups that are excluded from governance decide to break away and establish a separate state. As long as democracy and a free press are absent, there will be turmoil and violence. The only answer is to open up the political system. In addition, African countries must go back to the idea of the free-enterprise system that previously existed—when people (especially women) would bring produce to the market and freely buy and sell—not state-based economic organizations.

Apart from these grand singular-cause theories, the majority of experts recognize poverty as resulting from many interrelated causes, all of which must be addressed in an integrated fashion. Consider Paul Collier's views in his book *The Bottom Billion*.[4] According to Collier, the billion people at the bottom live in "trapped countries." He identifies four elements that cause countries to become trapped:

1. *Civil War*. A great number of the bottom billion have been or are currently experiencing civil war. Wars result from these countries having large numbers of young men who are unemployed and uneducated as well as the existence of ethnic imbalances.
2. *"Natural Resource Curse."* Almost a third of these countries rely on exporting some raw materials. They typically lack the skills to add value to these natural resources. These governments tend to be corrupt and don't hold democratic elections.
3. *Landlocked Countries*. Almost a third of these countries are land-locked and economically disadvantaged, and they are surrounded by "bad neighbors."
4. *Bad Governance*. About three-fourths of these countries are governed by autocratic or corrupt leaders.

SOLUTIONS TO POVERTY

Each contributing condition requires a specific solution. Collier favors legitimate military interventions in areas being torn apart by civil war. Countries with large amounts of natural resources should develop skills that raise the value of their exports and should not simply export raw

materials at world market prices. As for landlocked countries, they have
to work with neighboring port-based countries to build roads that will
give them access to ports. Bad governance is the hardest problem to
solve. During his years in power, Robert Mugabe ran Zimbabwe into the
ground while the rest of the world stood by helplessly.

Collier's chief recommendation to fight poverty is to "narrow the target and broaden the instruments." Narrowing the target means focusing
only on the one billion of the world's people (70 percent of whom are in
Africa) who are in countries that are failing. Broadening the instruments
means shifting focus from simply providing aid to offering an array of
policy instruments: better delivery of aid, occasional military intervention, international charters, and smarter trade policy.

What about foreign aid as a partial solution to the problems of the
poor? There are two experts who hold sharply different views on the
effectiveness of foreign aid. Jeffrey Sachs, author of *The End of Poverty*,
wants the West to be more generous and give substantially more foreign
aid to the poor countries.[5] On the other hand, William Easterly, in *The
White Man's Burden,* advances strong arguments against foreign aid.[6] He
describes Sachs as one of those big "top-down planners" who is never
embarrassed about the many failures of foreign aid. Some estimate that
as little as 15 percent of foreign aid reaches the deserving poor as a result
of high administrative expenses and corruption. The "top-down planning" of foreign aid relief agencies fails to provide information on variations in local needs for medicines and foods. Foreign aid also creates a
dependency that keeps countries from reaching for their own solutions.

Foreign aid hurts a country's private businesses that produce or sell
the same foreign aid items. Easterly sees the work of large foreign aid
bureaucracies and their vast expenditures and interventions to be largely
a failure. At the same time, Easterly acknowledges some good deeds of
these large foreign aid agencies, especially when they concentrate on
particular needs—like drilling and maintaining local wells, building

and maintaining local roads or sewage systems, or distributing medicine or food in particular places where they are needed.

The major problem of top-down planning is that huge agencies at the international and national level have to decide on the allocation of money to the different poverty-alleviation tools. They make their decision by setting priorities that reflect the overall conditions in the country. But from village to village, and city to city, the priorities may vary. This means that some communities receive more to spend on causes that are not important and other communities receive less than they need to spend.

This makes it desirable to add a "bottom-up planning approach" that engages all the communities to develop their own proposals and programs of need, which are then passed upward. The programs must meet certain criteria, such as taking a long view of what would develop the community, and explain the logic of the program. The need is to "Take the mountain into the valley." In *The Fortune at the Bottom of the Pyramid,* the late C. K. Prahalad eloquently describes how local innovation and financial assistance to the poor can incent the indigent to help themselves escape from poverty.[7]

A NOTE ON U.S. POVERTY

What about poverty in the United States? During Bill Clinton's presidency (1993–2001), the U.S. poverty rate averaged 11 percent.[8] In 2008, the poverty rate was 13.2 percent. The Great Recession followed and by November 2012, the U.S. poverty rate climbed to 16 percent, according to the U.S. Census Bureau, with more than 43.6 million Americans living in poverty, including almost 20 percent of American children.[9]

Tavis Smiley and Cornel West go further and claim that one out of every two Americans lives in poverty or near poverty. They define "near poverty" as a situation of people who live from paycheck to paycheck and where any interruption in their weekly paycheck has the potential to put them into poverty.[10] They believe that we have rendered the poor invisible to the rest of us.

President Ronald Reagan once remarked, "We fought a War on Poverty. Poverty won." Poverty in the U.S. is still winning, thirty years later.

Other developed nations have done better. The United States ranks 28th among all nations and its poverty level is even higher than that found in Russia, Poland, and South Korea.[11]

A family of four is considered poor if the family's income is below $23,850. About one-third of Americans experience occasional poverty, and about 20 percent experience poverty all the time. The poverty rate differs by race, age, education level, and economic, social, and demographic factors. The rate is highest among African-American minors. The problem is exacerbated by the high debt burden, the rise in oil prices, the collapse of housing prices, and the deindustrialization resulting from U.S. jobs moving abroad to China and elsewhere.

There is some debate about whether today's poor are really suffering, given that a family might have a car, a flat-screen TV, cell phones, and a computer with an Internet connection. The skeptics point out that Wal-Mart and other businesses have lowered the prices of clothes, TVs, bicycles, computers, and many other consumer goods. But this neglects the higher costs of education, health care, child care, electricity, gasoline, and so on. Many poor families barely make it from paycheck to paycheck and depend very much on payday loans (at a much higher interest rate) to pay bills. They carry a high debt burden and often have to cut their food purchases in the middle of the month, conserve on other things, and put some assets into a pawn shop to tide them over.

Clearly the living condition of the U.S. poor is propped up by food stamps (started during Franklin Roosevelt's presidency), Medicaid, housing vouchers, welfare payments, Social Security, legal assistance to the poor, Head Start programs to help children from birth to age 5 from low-income homes to prepare them for school, Pell grants to enable low-income students to go to college, and other government programs. There is increasing pressure to raise minimum wages, to create more manufacturing and other jobs, to increase worker training and skills, and to increase taxes on the rich to pay for the array of antipoverty programs. Tavis Smiley and Cornel West advance these and other ideas, such as creating more workplace day care centers, a public housing program for the homeless, and stronger unions.[12] How these proposals to reduce poverty will be utilized by a divided, indeed polarized, Congress is anyone's guess.

* * *

Given all these different approaches to helping the poor, I recommend the following:

- The best solutions will involve more than government solutions and NGO solutions. They will involve the private sector as well, working closely with government agencies and civic organizations.
- Much of the work of helping the poor lies in using tools to understand, influence, and assist the poor to participate in developing their own solutions.
- We need to link the big national picture of the poverty problem with the specific conditions found in each local situation.
- We should use the tools of social marketing planning, implementation, monitoring, and control. Social marketing aims to change or support behaviors that lead to results good for the people and for the society. I believe that social marketing as a tool has been missing in all the previous work on helping the poor.
- We must carefully consider whether it would make more sense for national governments to guarantee everyone a certain minimum income and do away with the many War on Poverty programs that only act as bandages to slow down the bleeding.

TWO

INCOME INEQUALITY
ON THE RISE

Our economy won't come back unless it comes back fair.

—JOSEPH STIGLITZ, *The Price of Inequality*

The poverty problem we examined in Chapter 1 is closely related to a wider problem—namely, the growing gap in the share of income going to the rich, the middle class, and the poor. One of the key issues in capitalism is whether it must inevitably lead to great and growing differences in personal income and wealth. Under capitalism, will the poor remain poor and will the rich acquire a growing share of income and wealth?

The grand idea of capitalism is that those with capital will apply it to create more wealth that will lead to more jobs and income for everyone. Not only will the wealthy benefit, but their wealth will "trickle down." All boats will rise. In recent times, however, wealth is more likely to "trickle up." A growing GDP no longer means that poverty falls. The wealthy become better off, and the others don't benefit very much, if at all. The rich use their lobbyists in Congress to write rules that end up in tax loopholes that benefit the already affluent. Big Politics has aligned with Big Business. Many wealthy individuals pay lower tax rates than those on normal salaries. Warren Buffett and Mitt Romney both pay lower tax rates than their secretaries, because capital gains are taxed at a lower rate. The difference is that Warren Buffett doesn't think it is right. Billionaire Buffett says that he and the rest of the super-rich are under-taxed.

Those defending the super-rich put forth many arguments for not taxing them more. One is that an economy attains a "Pareto optimal level" when no one can be made better off without making someone worse off.[1] Vilfredo Pareto argued that taking a dollar from a millionaire and giving it to a starving person to buy food does not mean that we've increased the amount of total satisfaction in the whole socioeconomic system. Because satisfaction is a subjective state, the millionaire could derive as much or more satisfaction from that dollar as the starving person spending it on food. The Pareto optimal is another defense for the rich remaining untouched and the poor remaining poor. Little wonder economics has been called the "dismal science."

Buffett has joined with Bill Gates to persuade the world's wealthiest individuals and their families to sign a Giving Pledge to dedicate the majority of their wealth to philanthropy to improve the lives of people.[2] So far 132 people have signed up, and their individual pledges are posted on a website for all to see. This organized approach to volunteering a share of one's wealth is unprecedented and bound to do much good.[3]

In addition, a growing group called Patriotic Millionaires in the U.S. has lobbied Congress to raise the taxes on the rich and to close tax loopholes. They believe that no millionaire should pay at a lower tax rate than middle-class Americans. They favor a more progressive tax on the rich in order to raise money to improve education, health, and infrastructure in this country.[4]

THOMAS PIKETTY ARRIVES ON THE SCENE

Thomas Piketty, a French economist who specializes in income distribution, argues in his book *Capital in the Twenty-First Century* that inequality will inevitably worsen under free market capitalism.[5] He asserts that capital owners will become increasingly dominant over those who only receive wages. To Piketty, the fundamental question is whether the rate of return to capital will be greater or less than the rate of growth of the world economy. Piketty claims that during the six decades between 1914 and 1973, the rate of economic growth exceeded the rate of return to capital and led to the material improvements in the lives of workers. This was the period of two world wars and a Great Depression that destroyed a lot of capital.[6] He sees this as a unique historical period that is not likely to be repeated. In the forty years since 1973, the rate of return to capital has exceeded the rate of economic growth, which has slowed down. Piketty says that the higher the rate of return to capital is in comparison to the rate of growth of the economy, the greater the inequality will be. He asserts that this is the more natural condition of capitalism and leads to growing inequality.

Piketty sees wealth today as rising faster than income. In the 1970s, the ratio of wealth to income was about 250 percent; nowadays it is about 500 percent. Income has slowed down because of slower productivity growth and slow population growth. Wealth has grown because of relative peace and heavy capital gains.[7]

The inevitable consequence is that the wealthy become dominant. The wealthy set their own pay or the company boards pay very generously. Each company board, in hiring a new CEO, feels it must pay as much or more than the competitive companies pay their CEO, rather than using the firm's earnings or share price or some other yardstick. In many sectors, especially in the financial sector, there is more collusion than real competition. The wealthy see their pay as describing their worth, and they rely on their wealth and political influence to defeat democratic measures to contain or tax them sufficiently. Democracy is therefore in danger of being destroyed by capitalism. Unless there is higher taxation on wealth and more regulation to promote real competition, democracy is subverted.[8]

HOW IS INCOME DISTRIBUTED?

Let's look more closely at the vastly different levels of incomes and wealth in different countries. Measured in terms of median income (which is a better measure than average income), Australia leads with $220,000, followed by Luxembourg, Belgium, France, Italy, the U.K., and Japan. The United States falls way down the list on this measure, with a median wealth of just $45,000. The remaining countries trail all the way down to the poorest of the poor.

Oxfam is an international charity focused on fighting poverty and empowering impoverished individuals around the world. It released a 2014 report containing the startling fact that the richest eighty-five people in the world are worth more than the poorest 3.5 billion.[9] "Our estimates suggest that the lower half of the global population possesses barely one percent of global wealth, while the richest 10 percent of adults own 86 percent of all wealth, and the top one percent account for 46 percent of the total," the report states. This means that we are living today in a time of wealth distribution similar to that of the pharaohs of ancient Egypt or the royal court of Louis XIV before the French Revolution.

About one percent of the U.S. population has extremely high incomes and wealth. Let's call these people the *super-rich*. This group consists largely of executives and managers; many come from the world of finance. In 2012, the average household in the bottom 90 percent of the income distribution earned about $30,997 while the average household in the top one percent earned $1,264,065 and for the top 0.1 percent about $6,373,782.[10] In 2012, $16.7 billion were paid to the top forty hedge fund managers and traders, which was equivalent to the wages of 400,000 ordinary workers.[11] This contrast highlights the excessive pay of the few.

Below the super-rich are the *affluent*, who are about 5 percent of the population. They enjoy discretionary income well beyond that needed for basic food, clothing, and shelter. They can take expensive vacations, eat at expensive restaurants, send their children to expensive colleges, and invest in capital growth for personal wealth and trusts.

Below them is the *middle class*. Capitalism created the middle class! Earlier times consisted of only the rich and the working poor. The middle class enjoys stable jobs and pleasant homes and can eat out and buy the latest appliances. At the same time, they have to be careful in their expenditures. Usually their income requires two working parents who are finding it harder to send their children to expensive colleges and who want to save enough to support their aging parents and themselves in case they incur heavy medical expenses. They hope that their pensions and homes hold up in value.

The middle class is becoming a myth for many people ever since the Great Recession. There are former professionals who now stock grocery shelves and retired persons whose savings have nearly disappeared. The Pew Research Center says that the middle class has fallen from 53 percent to 44 percent of the U.S. population.[12] Studies show that upward mobility in the United States is decreasing and is lower than in Britain, France, and a number of other Western countries. Given the low quality of U.S. public education and the lessening affordability of higher education, it is becoming harder to get into the middle class. By the time young people go to school and have their ability judged, their path in life has been set by their family and the economic circumstances that they are born into.

Below the middle class is the *working class,* whose jobs enable them to earn just enough to meet their bills and have enough for basic food, clothing, and shelter. If married, both partners are already working. Many are single-parent or single-person households, and some earn only a minimum wage.

Below the working class are the *poor,* who would not get enough food and shelter if it weren't for food stamps, the earned income tax credit (EITC), subsidized housing, and Medicaid. The U.S. Census Bureau reported that in 2012, 15 percent of Americans, or 46.5 million people, are poor. One in four American children are poor. Some argue that the poor of today are much better off than the poor of yesterday, because of Medicaid, unemployment insurance, food stamps, and other benefits. They probably have a TV set, running water, and a toilet in their home. Granting that "being poor" is a moving concept, it still doesn't make up for the fact that so many poor go hungry, lack a regular doctor, and cannot afford higher education or to hire a lawyer if they need one.

The problem of inequality and social justice occurs when there is a great distance between the earnings of the poor and the working class and the affluent and the super-rich. Consider that the poor make up the largest population group in the world. Jeffrey Sachs estimates that 5 billion of the 7 billion people living on the earth today are poor.[13] Something is wrong in human society or in human nature when 5 billion people don't have adequate food, clothing, and shelter while 2 billion people enjoy an appropriate or even a plentiful life.

And what about the super-rich? The labor economist Sylvia Allegretto estimates that in 2007, the six Walton family members on the Forbes 400 had a net worth equal to the bottom 30 percent of all Americans—that is, the 100 million Americans at the bottom.[14] These are six persons lucky enough to be born into the right family. They didn't do anything to create their wealth. They are simply the beneficiaries of the brilliance of Sam Walton who founded Wal-Mart. Should Sam Walton have been taxed at a much higher rate to prevent this great wealth from accumulating? Would Sam have worked this hard at the higher tax rate? These are tough questions without simple answers.

Let's look at some other interesting facts. Here is a list of the annual take-home pay of the top five U.S. CEOs in 2013, including salary, bonuses, stock, and stock options:[15]

1. Larry Ellison, Oracle $78.4 million (or $37,692
                                                an hour)[16]
2. Robert A. Iger, Walt Disney $34.3 million
3. Rupert Murdoch, 21st Century Fox $26.1 million
4. David M. Cote, Honeywell
   International $25.4 million
5. David N. Farr, Emerson Electric $25.3 million

The median pay going to CEOs is $10 million (aside from exceptions such as Tim Cook of Apple taking home $378 million in 2011). Michael Dorff attacked the whole system of high CEO pay. He says that during the period of the late 1940s to the late 1960s, CEOs were paid salaries. Then performance-related pay came into the system on the unproven argument that CEOs would work harder if they received performance pay. Dorff argues that pay for performance can lead to short-run planning and risky behavior. It has resulted in a dramatically increased proportion of profits going from the shareholders to the CEOs. Dorff advocates returning to straight salaries for CEOs.[17]

The pay to CEOs even pales compared to the pay received by the highest paid hedge fund managers. Here are the 2011 incomes of the three top hedge fund managers:[18]

1. Ray Dalio, Bridgewater Associates $3.9 billion
2. Carl Icahn, Icahn Capital
   Management $2.5 billion
3. James Simons, Renaissance
   Technologies $2.1 billion

Paul Krugman has noted that the top twenty-five hedge fund general partners made a combined $21 billion in 2013.[19] Doesn't the hedge fund pay system require some correction?

Now let's consider severance pay packages. General Electric's Jack Welch received a $417 million farewell package from GE's board upon retirement. William McGuire left UnitedHealth Group—in the midst of a stock option scandal—with a $286 million severance package. Are these severance pay packages right for the shareholders and workers?

Public companies are also generous in compensating their board directors. Many years ago, I received about $25,000 to attend individual board meetings, usually four a year. By 2013, the average annual total compensation per director (excluding the independent chairman) was $245,842, consisting of stock grants, option grants, cash fees, and other compensation).[20]

Not every CEO is greedy. Several CEOs managing top companies are satisfied with receiving total annual compensation under $6 million: Edward S. Lampert of Sears ($4.6 million), A. G. Lafley of P&G ($2 million), and Steve Ballmer, formerly of Microsoft ($1.2 million).[21] Given that these executives have the skills to manage huge companies, why are the other executives receiving such high pay?

One explanation for excessive CEO pay levels is an addiction to greed. These CEOs know they will never be hungry and they can acquire any material possessions they desire—personal airplanes, yachts, or several mansions. Sam Polk, who had accumulated a huge income, wrote how one day he regained his life by overcoming his wealth addiction. His manic drive for "more" no longer made any sense.[22]

Let's ask a simple hypothetical question. Suppose Larry Ellison, CEO of Oracle, suddenly feels overpaid with his yearly income of $78.4 million. He decides that he can live on $3.4 million and wants to give his Oracle employees higher pay so that they can pay down some debt on their credit cards, given that the average worker carried a credit card debt of $15,000 in 2012. Ellison decides to give a one-time gift of $10,000 to 7,500 of his employees to ease their credit card burden. Larry Ellison has made 7,500 families happier without sacrificing hardly anything in his own family's lifestyle. But readers may ask alternatively why the excessive income is not distributed to shareholders as dividends. Did the Oracle shareholders overpay the CEO?

If companies paid less to the excessively paid CEOs, would that cause the companies to underperform? There are probably enough hardworking and able managers who would be motivated and satisfied to be paid 50 times the average wage versus 200 times the average.

People clearly have different attitudes about the rightness or wrongness of extremely large differences in income and wealth. Here are some commonly held opinions:

"I am only concerned with whether I have equal opportunity and not with income differences."

"There will always be extreme differences in income. It is the survival of the fittest."

"High incomes are mostly the result of differences in ability that lead to differences in income."

"High incomes come from having the right parents. If you are born into a wealthy family, you will be brought up with more advantages and go to the right colleges and get excellent jobs, partly through your parents' connections."

"The super-rich have rigged the system to make us complacent by feeding us the 'candy' of television and other distractions so that we don't notice their thievery."

"From a social justice point of view, I think that the rich should be taxed proportionately higher than the average income earner."

I can imagine one system of income distribution that would be worse than today's. The worst would be if everyone was limited to getting the exact same income, regardless of age, family size, ability, effort, and other factors. There would be no incentive to work or to innovate. The system we have today of extreme income and wealth disparity has existed throughout most of history. Areas were run by a tribal leader or a king or queen who, along with close followers and courtiers, would amass great wealth. There was hardly a middle class. There was a peasant or working class, and most of the laborers were serfs or slaves living on a bare subsistence level.

But today, with not only newspapers and radio and television but also with Google and Facebook and YouTube and other digital media, more people are learning about the vast differences in the earnings of the median American household ($51,000) and the super-rich. For example, a *New York Times* article revealed that in 2012, the top one percent took more than one-fifth of the income earned by Americans. The top 10 percent took more than half of the country's total income in 2012.[23] That kind of vast income disparity gets noticed.

The rich have raced far ahead. In 2012, the incomes of the top one percent rose nearly 20 percent compared with a one percent increase for the remaining 99 percent. The median income of households in the top 5 percent stands at $318,052. The income of these highest-earning Americans has recovered completely from a fall after the financial crisis, compared with the 8 percent decline for the median American household.[24] The share of the highest income earners is close to its highest level in a century.[25]

DANGERS OF THE INEQUALITY

There is a growing concern about growing income inequality. Some level of income inequality is needed to propel growth. But most economists agree that high and growing income inequality will slow down the rate of economic growth. Those with low incomes often have poorer health and lower productivity. Growing income inequality frays social bonds and may lead to class conflict. The high level of youth unemployment can trigger social protests. Young people were a key force in the Arab Spring uprisings and the Occupy Wall Street protests. They see a shrinking economic pie and they receive a shrinking share of that pie. Widening income inequality raises deep questions about social justice and "class warfare." President Obama has declared that inequality is "the defining challenge of our age."

Income inequality is not only felt by the poor and the working class, but also by many members of the middle class. Many managers in the middle class wonder why top management has to be paid so much when they earn $100,000 or less. Some CEOs of smaller businesses who take home about $1 million to $5 million a year and have the skills to run much larger companies question the super payments of $10 million to $80 million a year to other executives.

Even when income inequality is excessively high, it can be reduced by redistribution payments. Economists use the Gini index as a measure of income inequality. The Gini index ranges from 0, representing perfect equality, to 100, where all income flows to one person. Germany's Gini index before any redistribution is 55. But redistribution programs are strong in Germany and the Gini index for Germany falls to 30 after redistribution is taken into account. By contrast, the United States has a lower Gini index of 47 before redistribution. But the U.S. has a weaker redistribution push, reducing its Gini index to 37.

A study involving scholars from the Harvard Business School and Duke University asked Americans which country they would rather live in. They were shown the income distribution of country A and B (and were not told the countries were actually Sweden and the United States). About 90 percent of Americans preferred to live in a country with the Swedish post-redistribution income distribution![26] Sweden uses redistribution to cut its Gini index from 45 to 22.[27] However, there is some evidence that too much redistribution may reduce growth. Some assert that Europe's slow growth rate is due to its high social costs.

Pope Francis of the Roman Catholic Church has complained about "the tyranny of unfettered capitalism." He said to the wealthy: "I ask you to ensure that humanity is served by wealth and not ruled by it."[28] In his January 1, 2014, message, he said that huge salaries and bonuses are symptoms of an economy based on greed and inequality and called for nations to narrow the wealth gap. Others have wondered whether the increased financial risk taking of "Casino Capitalism" will lift the lives of ordinary people or only fill the coffers of the rich. We begin to suspect the growth mantra that says "a rising tide lifts all the boats." We note the high dropout of workers from the labor force who have given up looking for work as if the earnings are too low to be worth the effort. The government doesn't even count them anymore as being unemployed.

From an economics point of view, we can assert that the high concentration of income and wealth leads to a reduced level of consumer demand, thereby continuing the economic malaise. The working and middle class meet their needs by using credit cards to pile up more debt than they can repay, thus laying the conditions for an eventual boom and bust. With consumers lacking enough earnings, businesses are cautious and keep their production and employment at a low level.

The social fabric is further hurt because both parents have to work and give less time to their children. Money stress leads to divorce and the growing number of single-parent households. Working-class parents before 2008 were tempted to buy a home saddled with a substantial mortgage in the expectation that home value would increase. All this ended in a terrible bubble of falling home prices and foreclosures when some people simply walked away from their homes. This meant that their college-age children couldn't go to college unless they took substantial student loans. Student loan debt has grown to over $1 trillion. We are finding that education and health care costs are growing at rates exceeding income and wealth growth for the working and middle class.

I would assert that the growing income disparity is not only a disaster for the poor, but also a threat to the rich. Poverty breeds broken families, crime and criminal organizations, beggars, prostitution, mass immigration, social protest movements, and failed states.[29] Go to certain cities in Latin America or South Africa where the high crime rates force the wealthy to live in gated communities or in walled homes or to even hire their own militias.

Too often the discussion is cast as a condemnation of either the "idle poor" or the "heartless rich." But most workers are not the "idle poor" and most rich people are not the "heartless rich." This is dealing in stereotypes rather than addressing the real issues.

One of the best indications that some wealthy people are becoming concerned about growing income inequality is the May 27, 2014, Inclusive Capitalism Conference held in London and attended by Bill Clinton, Prince Charles, Christine Lagarde, and other elite who control a third of the world's wealth.[30] The aim of the conference was "to discuss the need for a more socially responsible form of capitalism that benefits everyone" and that is less likely to produce economic disasters like the Great Recession.

The elite do not want to face a global uprising of the disenfranchised against capitalism. Dominic Barton of McKinsey, addressing his elite conference peers, warned that "there is a growing concern that if the fundamental issues revealed in the crisis remain unaddressed and the system fails again, the social contract between the capitalist system and the citizenry may truly rupture, with unpredictable but severely damaging results." In pondering solutions, the elite group wanted practical solutions. Barton hoped that the government would refrain from intervening with business in what he called "unproductive ways." "I think that it is imperative for us to restore faith in capitalism and in free markets," he said.[31]

The elite group did not want to see "increased regulation" and "greater state" involvement in the economy, nor did it seek punishment for responsible parties. In the end, this group decided to invest in a public relations campaign "to influence political and business opinion."[32]

This is a rather weak response to such a serious problem. The fact is that capitalism had failed to produce a "golden age" for the vast majority of the world's population. The Inclusive Capitalism Conference came up with ideas such as more job training and more partnering with small and medium-size businesses. But those attending refused to consider a whole range of more basic solutions to reduce the growing differences in incomes and wealth.

POLICIES FOR REDUCING THE GREAT DIFFERENCES IN INCOMES

We need to acknowledge that much of the great disparity in income comes from globalization and technology and differences in education, none of which we can do much about except through changing government tax policy. Globalization means that companies will move production to countries with lower labor costs. Technology helps companies replace labor with capital when labor becomes too expensive. And educational differences go a long way to explain the great difference in earnings within a country.

Yet there are a number of measures that can be taken to reduce the great differences in incomes.

Raise the Minimum Wage

One solution is to raise workers' pay through establishing a higher minimum wage. In the United States, there is growing pressure to raise the national minimum wage, which has stayed too long at $7.25. Thirteen states have already raised their state minimum wage above $7.25. The state of Washington set it at $9.32. The Democratic Party advocates raising the hourly minimum wage to $10.10 by 2016 and thereafter indexing the minimum wage to inflation. Germany and Britain have raised their minimum wage to $11.30 an hour. Denmark is at $20.30 an hour. In 2014, Switzerland, which does not have a statutory minimum wage, rejected a proposal to set the minimum wage at $25 an hour, which would have been the highest in the world. (Interestingly, 90 percent of Swiss workers already exceed that wage.)

In my opinion, the U.S. minimum wage is a disgrace. Yet those opposed to raising it cite two possible undesirable consequences. First, some small businesses, which hardly make a profit paying workers $7.25 an hour, are likely to close shop at a higher minimum wage. Second, employers will search for other ways to replace labor with capital. Both of these consequences may have the effect of reducing the number of jobs, but paying more to those who are still employed.

I'll have more to say about raising the minimum wage in Chapter 3.

Make the Tax System More Progressive

We are living at a time when the extreme income gap is making daily headlines. The most important civil issue facing the nation may be middle-class stagnation and the growing number of poor people.

In 2014, the U.S. Congress chose not to renew unemployment benefits for another year to the long-term unemployed, even though the government hasn't done enough to create jobs for these people. In addition, the food stamp program is being reduced, resulting in an average 7 per-cent decrease in benefits for about 45 million people. As a result, we hear of single mothers—who were once receiving unemployment benefits but no longer are—now learning that food stamps will be cut, so they will have to go to soup kitchens to feed their family.

It is not surprising that we hear new cries for increasing taxes on the rich. Bill de Blasio, New York City's mayor, proposed taxing the "very wealthy" just a little more in order to be able to provide full-day, univer-sal pre-K as well as after-school programs. "Those earning between $500,000 and $1 million . . . would see their taxes increase by an average of $973 a year. That's less than three bucks a day—about the cost of a small soy latte at your local Starbucks."[33]

This leads to the larger idea of a progressive tax system that would establish higher tax rates for higher income brackets. The U.S. tax sys-tem is already progressive. Here are the tax rates in 2013:

Tax rate	Taxable income
10 percent	$0 to $17,850
15 percent	over $17,850 to $72,500
25 percent	over $72,500 to $146,400
28 percent	over $146,400 to $223,050
33 percent	over $223,050 to $398,350
35 percent	over $398,350 to $450,000
39.6 percent	over $450,000

The question can be raised: Is the maximum tax rate of 39.6 percent a high enough tax on the rich, given the growing level of income in-equality?

Consider that in 1939, the U.S. top tax rate was 75 percent. It rose to 91 percent during WWII for incomes over $200,000, which was a high income at that time. In 1964, the highest tax rate was lowered to 70 percent. Starting in 1981, President Reagan managed to lower the maximum rate from 70 percent to 50 percent and subsequently down to 38.5 percent. (Reagan has been praised by the right as a tax-cutting president, but he actually raised taxes eleven times.) During President Clinton's term (1993–2001), the top marginal rate was raised to 39.6 percent. Under President George W. Bush, the maximum tax rate was lowered to 35 percent. His deep tax cuts were scheduled to expire at the end of 2010, but they became permanent. Many people believe that the full Bush-era tax cuts were the single biggest contributor to the deficit in the subsequent decade, reducing revenues by about $1.8 trillion between 2002 and 2009. During the 2008–2011 fiscal cliff confrontation, the top tax rate was raised back to 39.6 percent.

Close Offshore Tax Havens

Profits earned by U.S. companies are subject to a 35 percent tax rate. Clearly, U.S. companies want to reduce their taxes if possible. There are three approaches they use to accomplish this.

The first is to set up a U.S. company subsidiary in Bermuda, the Cayman Islands, or Ireland. A U.S. company making a printing machine for $10,000 in Chicago might sell it to a Miami printing company for $12,000. It would have to pay a 35 percent tax on the $2,000 of profit—namely, $700. Instead, it could sell the printing machine to its own subsidiary in Bermuda for $10,000 at no profit. Then its Bermuda subsidiary can sell it to the Miami printing company for $12,000, making a $2,000 profit in Bermuda. But Bermuda doesn't tax profits (or taxes substantially less than the U.S.). In this way, the U.S. government lost $700 in taxes on this transaction alone. It is estimated that 362 of the Fortune 500 companies operate tax haven subsidiaries. The U.S. government is losing a great amount of corporate tax revenue, requiring the American public to either pay higher taxes or face reduced social welfare, education, and health benefits.

The second tax avoidance scheme is called "inversion." If an American company can show that some percentage of its shares are owned by another company abroad, it doesn't have to pay U.S. taxes on this amount. For example, the Walgreens company might buy an Irish drugstore chain and pay for it by issuing more shares of its stock. Walgreens of Ireland would have to pay taxes to Ireland, but Ireland's taxes are considerably lower than U.S. taxes.

The U.S. government needs to worry about a third possibility where a U.S. corporation starts thinking about moving its headquarters out of the country. The consulting firm Accenture began as a U.S. company, then moved to the Cayman Islands, went public in 2002, and then moved to Ireland because of its lower taxes.[34] Eaton Corporation moved its headquarters from Cleveland to Dublin, saving $160 million a year in taxes. So far, some sixty U.S. companies were "never here" or have been using inversion to avoid U.S. taxes. Not only do these companies substantially reduce their taxes, but in addition they are less burdened by the endless growth in U.S. government regulations that now cover 169,301 pages.[35]

Gabriel Zucman, an economics professor at the London School of Economics and a protégé of Thomas Piketty, wrote a short book on tax evasion called *The Missing Wealth of Nations*. According to the *New York Times*, Zucman estimated that $7.6 trillion, or 8 percent of the world's personal financial wealth, rests in tax havens as hidden money.[36] If this money could be taxed, more than $200 billion a year could be added to tax revenues.

Zucman went further and estimated that 20 percent of all U.S. corporate profits are shifted offshore, with the result that these corporations manage to pay a corporate tax rate of 15 percent rather than the officially correct rate of 35 percent. U.S. corporations have accumulated $1.95 trillion outside of the United States.[37] U.S. companies don't pay U.S. taxes on profits earned abroad as long as that money remains abroad, often in

Bermuda, Ireland, Luxembourg, the Netherlands, and Switzerland. In 2013, Apple earned $54.4 billion abroad, IBM $52.3 billion, and Microsoft $76.4 billion. Proposals have been made to either lower corporate taxes to 25 percent or less or to change the tax code to require that these profits be invested in U.S.-located banks.

Zucman recommended that the U.S. and other nations prepare a global registry of personal and corporate wealth (just like there is a global registry of real estate holdings) and force the banks to disclose their holdings. The United States passed the 2010 Foreign Account Tax Compliance Act to enable the Internal Revenue Service to put pressure on foreign banks to disclose accounts held by American residents and corporations. In 2012, the U.S. imposed a $1.9 billion fine on HSBC, a British bank, for poor controls on money laundering. Fines have also been set on Barclays, ING, and Standard Chartered.

In 2010, the Republican House, under the influence of the Tea Party, cut the U.S. Internal Revenue Service (IRS) budget by 14 percent, resulting in a sharply reduced staff, less tax law enforcement, and weaker taxpayer service. Whereas in 2010, the IRS was able to audit 30 percent of income tax returns, in 2013 it audited only 24 percent. This means that the government collected less revenue that could have been used to build roads, clean our air and water, improve our health care, and carry out other vital government tasks.[38]

In summary, the U.S. maximum tax rate for a married couple was very high during WWII, then subsequently dropped from 70 percent to 50 percent to 38.5 percent to 35 percent before going back up to the current level of 39.6 percent. The Republicans consistently pushed for lower taxes, especially for the rich, on the theory that people need a strong incentive to work harder.

An entirely different tax philosophy operates in Scandinavian countries, where the maximum tax rate is 70 percent in Sweden and 72 percent in Denmark. The Scandinavian countries take care of their citizens' education and health from birth to death. There is little chance of a medical calamity bankrupting a Scandinavian family and families don't have to save as much for their future retirement.

In 2014, under President Francois Hollande, France established the highest marginal tax rate of 75 percent on individuals earning an income of over one million euros. The implication is that one million euros a year is a sufficient salary for any person and above that, the state should take 75 percent. Of course, this has led to outcries from the business community, and even France's soccer teams have threatened to leave the country.

I would add two optional features that might increase the acceptance of this 75 percent level. As option one, the tax money collected could be put into a separate government fund to help improve the education of poor students. Or option two, the money could go into a nonprofit foundation that supports a variety of social causes, and each family can even specify which category of causes it wishes to support.

The International Monetary Fund (IMF) has now taken aim at income inequality. Christine Lagarde, head of the IMF, is factoring in income inequality when deciding on financing programs for member states. A 2014 IMF staff paper said that "income inequality can be of macroeconomic concern for country authorities, and the fund should accordingly seek to understand the macroeconomic effects of inequality."[39]

What would a higher tax rate on the rich do to their incentive to work and earn income? Conservatives warn that talented CEOs, financiers, athletes, and movie stars would work less and we would suffer from a lower level of talent and output in these sectors. They claim that if high earners work less and start fewer businesses, the number of jobs would decrease, unemployment would increase, and average incomes will fall. They add that needed philanthropy would decline and long-term investment in infrastructure would dry up. They rail against "class warfare" that would "make everyone poorer." So why would we put any higher taxes on the rich than 39.6 percent?

Of course, there is no evidence to support this argument. When the U.S. government charged high marginal tax rates on the rich, we often had both high employment and high incomes. There were more periods of prosperity in the United States under the left-leaning Democratic Party than under the right-leaning Republican Party. We can't assume all high-income earners behave and react in the same way. I remember meeting a CEO of a large cereal company who confided to me that he was having so much fun running the company that he would have gladly managed his company for $1 a year. Mayor Michael Bloomberg, who over a twelve-year period brought New York City to a high level of prosperity, insisted on taking only $1 a year salary because he had all the money he needed to be satisfied.

I believe that both corporate executives and entrepreneurs are motivated primarily by three things: power, independence, and creativity. I don't believe that increases in the marginal tax rate would have a major downward impact on GDP, but that can be debated. Economic theory suggests one view on this subject. The law of diminishing returns says that further increments of income tend to produce diminishing returns or satisfaction. The law suggests that making an extra $10,000 will improve the well-being of a worker more than losing $10,000 would reduce the well-being of a millionaire. One study indicates that well-being increases as incomes approach $75,000 a year, but beyond that it does not consistently produce higher levels of personal happiness.[40] We can assume that it's easier for a rich person to give up the last $10,000 than a poor person.

Raising the tax rate on the rich may be an almost impossible task when we consider that it would have to be passed by Congress. Politicians get into office by being able to raise money. A new Republican representative must raise $500,000 a year just to give to the Republican

Party, aside from what he or she must raise to run his or her own campaign. Most of the money comes from those who are wealthy rather than from small contributions from the working and middle class. Politicians have little choice but to curry the rich and vote for what the wealthy want. And the wealthy, by and large, do not want to pay higher taxes.

Given that the rich are getting a growing share of the GDP, this means that less money is available for the poor and even the working class. This lack of purchasing power in the hands of the average citizen in turn slows down economic growth and leads to further immiseration of the poor. This is partly what led to Occupy Wall Street. The Occupy movement went from some seventy-five people demonstrating in a small Manhattan park to tens of thousands demonstrating in hundreds of cities in eighty countries, all in one month. We can expect more protest movements and political clashes in the future. In the past, these kinds of protesters were labeled "communists," and the wealthy managed to have them hounded or imprisoned. I don't see how substantially higher taxes on the rich can be passed politically without evoking another period of Red Scare and the Republican charge of the Democrats starting "class warfare."

Cap the Ratio of Top Executive Pay to Worker Pay

In 2010, Congress passed a rule requiring public companies to disclose the ratio of the CEO pay to the median compensation at the company. The objective was to help shareholders compare pay practices across companies. President Obama offered a specific proposal for holding down the high pay of executives. He held that executive pay should be related to the minimum federal wage.

At the time, his own $400,000 salary was twenty-seven times the minimum federal wage of $7.25. If the minimum wage rose to $10.10, his salary would be twenty times the minimum wage. He suggested that companies that do business with the federal government should not have their top executives paid in excess of 20 to 1, as the ratio of executive-to-worker compensation. This would mean the government would stop doing business with Oracle (1,284 to 1), General Electric (491 to 1), and AT&T (339 to 1). Although this proposal would be currently impractical, it captures the seed of an idea for limiting excessively high pay in the federal and private sector.[41] The state of Rhode Island is considering not buying from companies that pay their executives more than thirty-two times the lowest-paid worker.

Another idea would be to let companies pay whatever they want to pay their CEOs—but then tax corporations 50 percent to 70 percent on take-home pay in excess of a given ratio of CEO pay to median workers' pay.

The European Commission is actively encouraging member countries to consider pay-cap policies. Each public company is advised to take into account the ratio of top executive pay to average employee earnings. Companies should consider the impact of high executive pay on the long-run sustainability of the company. The EU is considering banning banker bonuses of more than twice the level of fixed pay, especially after seeing the hefty bonuses given by some of the major European banks.[42]

Plug the Tax Loopholes

There are many tax loopholes and deductions that collectively are worth more than $1 trillion and are largely benefiting the rich. Tax loopholes are not illegal, but they present a clear advantage to rich Americans without offering any offsetting advantages to poor Americans. These loopholes, along with the deregulation of Wall Street, made the rich richer and made the Great Recession inevitable. They also resulted in multibillions lost to the government that might otherwise have helped reduce the huge U.S. annual deficit. Ralph Nader, America's leading consumerist critic, holds that he would like to see all income from wages, dividends, capital gains, and rents taxed at the same rate to eliminate loopholes. Here are three major tax loopholes.[43]

1. *Capital Gains Tax Rate.* People who invest in securities for more than one year and then sell the securities were formerly taxed at 15 percent rather than at their normal income tax rate. The capital gains tax rate was raised to 20 percent plus another 3.8 percent temporary (or 23.8 percent). The purpose of this tax law is to encourage investors to stay in securities they believe in rather than switch their stock holdings frequently. The problem is that most wealthy people basically put their money into securities that they hold for over a year; therefore their effective tax rate on capital gains is 20 percent to 23.8 percent. This contrasts to wage earners who are taxed on their income anywhere up to 35 percent. It came out during Mitt Romney's run for president in 2012 that he had earned $13.7 million in 2011 but his tax rate was only 14.1 percent of his income. Financier Warren Buffett said that he was embarrassed to pay only a 15 percent tax on his income, a rate substantially lower than his secretary's tax rate on her income.[44] Buffett has advocated for a higher tax rate on top income earners who benefit from paying taxes at a lower rate on capital investments than regular earnings. This loophole is estimated to have cost the U.S. Treasury $457 billion between 2011 and 2015.

There is also an effort to end capital gains treatment for "carried interest." Carried interest is a share of any profits that the general partners of private equity and hedge funds receive as compensation, despite not contributing any initial funds. This method of compensation seeks to motivate the general partner (i.e., fund manager) to work toward improving the fund's performance. Traditionally, the amount of carried interest comes to around 20 percent of the fund's annual profit. While all funds tend to have a small management fee, the fee is meant to only cover the costs of managing the fund, with the exception of compensating the fund manager. Carried interest is meant to serve as the primary source of income for the general partner.[45]

The criticism is that putting a capital gains tax of only 15 percent or 20 percent on carried interest is another example of a preferential treatment of income tax mostly going to the very rich. The general partner of a hedge fund should pay an ordinary tax on this income because it is a reward for his labor in managing the fund, not for his capital.

2. *Home Mortgage Interest Deduction.* Anyone buying a home with a mortgage is allowed to deduct the mortgage interest payment from his tax bill. The purpose of this deduction is to encourage more home ownership on the notion that people owning homes (instead of renting) will be more rooted in their communities and care more for their communities. (Note that most other industrialized nations do not offer this deduction and people still buy homes.) This loophole is estimated to have cost the U.S. Treasury $464 billion between 2011 and 2015. It amounts to non-homeowners (i.e., renters) subsidizing homeowners. A homeowner with an income exceeding $200,000 gets an annual tax benefit of more than $2,200. He gets another mortgage tax benefit if he owns a second home, which primarily benefits wealthy people, who are the most likely to own another home. Furthermore, most of these high-income homes are in California and the Northeast, thereby giving a benefit that is geographically disproportionate.

3. *Tax on Foreign Earnings by U.S. Companies.* Companies that operate globally are able to avoid a tax on foreign income as long as they do not bring the income into the United States. In 2013, the

nation's top 1,000 companies reported $2.1 trillion in such earn-ings.[46] Companies such as Apple, GE, Pfizer, Merck, and others keep their money in offshore tax havens. If they brought this money into the U.S., the effective tax rate would be 35 percent. By not bringing it into the U.S., their stockholders are receiving no benefit from this money in dividends, nor is the company able to use this income to buy back its stock. Apple, for example, is (ironically) even considering raising money by issuing bonds to get the cash to pay higher dividends to its stockholders or buy back Apple stock. Meanwhile, the U.S. Treasury forgoes taxes on Apple's foreign income. One would think that the government should lower the tax rate on foreign-held corporate income to 10 or 20 percent if it would bring back much of this money to invest in the United States.

The problem may be getting even worse. Some U.S. compa-nies are thinking of reincorporating in another country where the corporate tax rate is lower. For example, Pfizer—the largest pharmaceutical firm in the United States—is considering buying AstraZeneca, another Big Pharma firm, and reincorporating the combined company in the United Kingdom. This move is called "inversion": Fifty U.S. companies have used inversion to avoid paying U.S. taxes in the past thirty years, and twenty of them have done so in the past two years. The U.S. is acting to prevent this loophole, especially for U.S. companies whose revenue is more than 80 percent in the U.S.[47]

Improve Transfer Payment Programs

Transfer payments represent money given by the government to its citi-zens. Examples include certain kinds of tax credits, Social Security, un-employment compensation, welfare, and disability payments. Here are two areas in which transfer payments could be made more equitable:

- *Strengthen the earned income tax credit.* The U.S. runs a large cash-transfer program to help the poor, which cost $61 billion in 2010. It provides up to $3,305 a year to low-income working families with one child and up to $6,143 for those with three or more children. The program has not been extended to help childless people who have very low incomes. Broadening the tax credit might make it possible to do away with food stamps and a miscellaneous set of other props aimed at providing a decent living for all.

- *Apply a stronger "means test" before making transfer payments.* I remember a wealthy person complaining about receiving a Social Security check for $3,500 each month. Although he is legally entitled to it because of his long history of putting money into the Social Security fund, he says that he shouldn't be getting it. Federal transfer payments should not go to people who have a good income or substantial wealth. Too many people who are unemployed claim and receive disability benefits who are not actually disabled. Social Security payments should be subject to a means test.

POLICIES FOR REDUCING THE GREAT DIFFERENCES IN WEALTH

We need to address a separate problem—namely, the great differences in wealth distribution, not just income distribution. The top one percent of income earners take home 25 percent of the total income in a year. But the wealthiest one percent of households holds 40 percent of the nation's wealth.[48] The wealthiest 10 percent of households holds 70 percent of the nation's wealth. *Forbes* reported there were 1,211 billionaires in 2011, a 20 percent increase from 982 in 2010. By investing this wealth, the super-rich further increase the highly skewed distribution of wealth.

According to the 2014 report of the Russell Sage Foundation, the median household wealth in America has substantially fallen in recent years.[49] Household wealth consists of the value of one's home, savings, and stocks and bonds, less debt of the median household in the U.S. The wealth of the median household in 2003 was $87,992, then rose in 2007 to $98,872, then fell in 2009 to $70,801, and in 2013 fell to $56,335. One can see how a major illness can easily wipe out the $56,335 wealth of a median American household.

Why is the high concentration of wealth a problem? Essentially it goes against the grain of a democratic society. In a democratic society, each qualified person should have one vote. But today, wealthy families have a disproportionate influence on the voting outcome. The super-rich behave more like oligarchs because of their ability to influence public policy. Are we living in a democracy or are we living in a plutocracy?

Recognize further that most of today's wealthiest people are wealthy by inheritance, not by contribution. Yet they are able to supply conservative candidates with a great amount of money for their election campaigns. The *Huffington Post* reported that billionaire Charles Koch pledged to give $40 million to unseat Barack Obama in the 2012 presidential election, while his brother David Koch pledged $20 million.[50]

The Supreme Court decided in the Citizens United case that a corporation could be called a "person" and, under "free speech" protection, create or give substantial sums of money to new nonprofit organizations to spread conservative views. Wealthy families and wealthy corporations, by giving heavy donations to conservative candidates, have a much greater voice in influencing who become our legislators and how they will vote. Working-class families lack the money to personally influence elections and can rely only on their shrinking unions to exercise some counter influence. The bottom line is that great extremes of income and wealth can diminish or destroy the power of the people to vote for the best candidates.

What can be done to reduce the great concentration of wealth? First, we have to put heavier taxes on the passage of estates to their heirs. Today, the estate of a super-rich person is exempt from a tax on the first

$5 million given to each heir. The tax rate on the rest of the estate is 55 percent. This rate can be raised even higher to reduce the concentration of wealth. Warren Buffett sagely observed that "a very rich person should be able to leave his kids enough to do anything but not enough to do nothing." This captures the spirit of what amount of money should be passed on to one's heirs.

The excessive compensation plans set up by companies for their senior executives is another area for reform. Buffett has been on the right side of this issue, but he flip-flopped when it came to Coca-Cola's executive compensation plan. Buffett owns over 9 percent of Coca-Cola's shares and is the largest investor. Another Coca-Cola shareholder charged that "the company expects that the 2014 plan will award a mix of 60 percent options, 40 percent full value shares, resulting in the issuance of 340 million Coca-Cola shares" that would transfer around $13 billion from shareholders to management. This shareholder saw this as an "outrageous grab."[51]

In the past, Buffett has come out against excessive executive compensation. At a 2009 meeting, for example, Buffett stated that he hoped institutional investors would "speak out on the most egregious cases."[52] However, in this case, Buffet decided to abstain from voting against Coca-Cola's new compensation plan because he didn't want to discourage the company's senior management, for whom he had great respect. This in spite of the fact that Buffett once said that stock options amount to giving away "free lottery tickets" and should be minimized.[53] Many people were disappointed that Buffett didn't have the courage to carry out his convictions.

Huge bonuses paid to top executives also skew the unequal concentration of wealth. These bonuses are often wildly out of balance with the actual contribution of the top executives to the company's profits. However, a few CEOs have declined the bonuses that they were entitled to. Virginia Rometty, CEO of IBM, was to collect a bonus of $8 million based on the company's performance and decided to turn it down. Barclays CEO, Antony Jenkins, turned down his bonus of $2.8 million for the second year in a row, saying, "It would not be right" to accept it. Similarly, Stephen Hester of the Royal Bank of Scotland turned down his annual performance bonuses.[54] These people could be said to have a reasonable sense of what's fair and proportionate.

Despite having so much in the way of advantages to help them boost their fortunes, many of the wealthy are bitter about proposals for higher taxes. Billionaire investor Tom Perkins of the venture capital firm Kleiner Perkins Caufield & Byers lamented public criticism of the "one percent" and compared it to the Nazi attacks on the Jews. Stephen Schwarzman of the Blackstone Group said that eliminating tax loopholes was "like when Hitler invaded Poland in 1939." These plutocrats react with a mix of paranoia and megalomania rather than thinking deeply about the problem that excessive wealth poses for the overall economy.[55] They are also outrageously out of line in their metaphors.

There is a whole industry involved in helping the super-wealthy hold on to their wealth beyond the last living member and even down to their grandchildren's grandchildren. South Dakota has pioneered "dynasty trusts" to help rich families escape estate taxes forever. In January 2013, Congress allowed families to set up a trust of $5 million that would have iron-clad secrecy. Lawyers have invented more complicated strategies to protect much larger fortunes.[56]

This again raises the question of whether higher estate taxes will lead to more avoidance and also cause talented people to work less hard or threaten to leave the country. I would argue that there are a great many talented civic-minded people waiting to move up the wealth ladder and take their place. The major issue, of course, is who would receive the redistributed wealth? Will it ultimately be used by government to increase wages and jobs? Or will it go into more defense spending and more bureaucracies?

We also need to look at other wealth sources and whether they need some trimming. For example, the country may be too generous in its subsidies to those who search for oil. Exxon Mobil took home a net income of $30 billion in 2012. Boards of directors might be too generous in the compensation packages that they set up for CEOs for take-home pay. Not long ago, the average CEO's take-home pay was twenty to forty times that of the average worker's income. Today, the average CEO may take home 300 times the pay of the average worker in his/her company. If the top guy gets that much, consider then what has to be paid to the company's vice presidents? This means that the expense of managing a major American company is top heavy in relation to its foreign competitors. For example, a Japanese CEO's take-home pay is more on the order 100 times the average worker's, rather than 300 times as in the United States.

Is there any realistic way to cap wealth accumulation? French economist Thomas Piketty holds that wealth inequity keeps growing because in this period "the rate of return on capital . . . is higher than the economy's growth rate."[57] He sees income from capital continuing to exceed income from wages and salaries as a worldwide phenomena. His preferred solution is "a global tax on wealth combined with higher rates of tax on the largest incomes." Wealth or capital would include real assets: land, houses, natural resources, office buildings, factories, machines, software, patents, stocks, and bonds. Households would have to declare their net worth to the tax authorities and pay a levy of one percent (for households with a net worth of between $1 million and $5 million) and 2 percent (for those worth more than $5 million). Piketty adds that even a steeper progressive tax of 5 percent to 10 percent on wealth above one billion euros would help break up such fortunes. In the United States, this would mean that the 16,000 people (the top hundredth of one percent) who have a combined net worth of $6 trillion would pay substantial taxes, and the money would hopefully be used to improve the education and health of the U.S. population.

Piketty recognizes problems with his intriguing proposal. First, the wealthy would scream that it would reduce incentives and innovation.

(Piketty doesn't believe that innovation will be hurt.) Second, this proposal would never be proposed, nor passed, because politicians are too dependent on the wealthy for their reelection. Third, the wealthy would transfer their wealth to other countries where this wealth tax did not exist. (They wouldn't transfer it to Spain, which has a wealth tax of 2.5 percent of assets.) All countries would have to pass such a wealth tax, which is clearly a utopian idea. Piketty is realistic, but offers his proposal as a standard against which to judge other proposals for curbing the growth of wealth inequity.

World Bank economist Branko Milanovic said of Piketty's *Capital in the Twenty-First Century*: "We are in the presence of one of the watershed books in economic thinking." Paul Krugman has said that it "will be the most important economics book of the year—and maybe of the decade."[58] Krugman thinks that Piketty's book has the potential of creating a monumental change in public attitudes toward growing income inequality.[59] The publicity that the book is receiving is making people aware that all great wealth is not the result of meritocracy, where great wealth is earned and deserved. Much of the income of the wealthy is not coming to them on the claim that they are "job creators." Much of their income is coming from the assets they own or their inheritance.

Piketty's book is now worrying the rich because they have not been able to tear down its premises. They rely on name-calling by claiming it is "Marxist" or "collectivist" or "Stalinistic." The rich are on the run politically and will use their money to confuse the public as much as possible regarding the real issues. One unsolved mystery is how it can be that so many Americans who are poor, working class, or even middle class identify their interests with the political party whose whole basis is to defend the interests of the super-rich.

The real challenge is to convince the super-rich that paying higher taxes would benefit them as well as the general public. Arguments can be used that roads and infrastructure will be improved, workers will have more money to spend on the businesses owned by the rich, and the public will think that the tax system is fairer and be willing to comply more readily. If the government can demonstrate that its operations are efficient and that their tax money is going to the right causes, people will be more willing to pay their fair share of taxes. In the end, is it better to move toward a budget calling for preserving tax loopholes, cutting taxes, and reducing investments in education, health, and infrastructure or to develop a system that raises more money through a fair and efficient tax system and uses the money to improve the lives of people?

* * *

Clearly, a whole set of interesting solutions exists to reduce the sharp differences between the earnings of the super-rich and the other groups—solutions that are not likely to damage incentives or productivity. The problem is not one of sound economics. It is the way politics interferes with economics and allows the rich and their publicists to confuse average citizens as to what lies in their true interests and in the country's long-term interest.

Let's return to our initial question about whether capitalism is intrinsically destined to produce little for the poor and extreme incomes and wealth for the few. This may well be the tendency of free market or unregulated capitalism. But if so, capitalism could contain the seeds of its own destruction. Why? Capitalism depends on consumers having enough money to buy the goods and services that the capitalist economic machine produces. Without rising real income in the pockets of the majority of the citizens, the result is overstocks of goods, slowdowns in investment and production, and a rising unemployment rate. The amount of joblessness may reach a point of inspiring an uprising and attack on not only the wealthy, but on capitalism itself.

Ultimately, capitalism will be judged on the degree to which it improves the lives of all its citizens. A good place to start would be with a fairer tax regime on wealth.

THREE

WORKERS UNDER SIEGE

Have a heart that never hardens, and a temper that never tires, and a touch that never hurts.

— CHARLES DICKENS

Has capitalism been good for the working class? This question was central in the battle between capitalism and communism. Communism held that the workers were exploited under capitalism. Those supporting capitalism say that workers around the world have better lives because of capitalism.

Karl Marx developed a labor theory of value—that is, all value came from the worker's time and effort in production and distribution. Even capital that is used in production represents the past work of labor. Marx describes capitalism as having an institutional framework in which a small minority, the capitalists, has a monopoly on the means of production. Workers cannot survive except by working for capitalists, and the state reinforces this inequality of power. There is a *reserve army of unemployed workers* who depress the potential earnings of employed workers who are exploited.

Worker exploitation was vivid during the Industrial Revolution in Britain. Coal miners worked ten hours a day, six days a week, coming home exhausted and dying at an early age. Factory workers included young children, who never had time for schooling, working at assembly lines, doing the same work day after day, and being paid a pittance.

Worker exploitation was also vivid in the United States, especially with new immigrants working under sweatshop conditions and migrant workers working for pennies on farms. Consider the following two major books:

The Jungle (1909) by Upton Sinclair
- Sinclair described the hard lives of immigrants in Chicago and exposed the health violations and unsanitary practices in the American meatpacking industry during the early twentieth century. The book depicts working-class poverty, the absence of social programs, harsh, unpleasant living and working conditions, and a hopelessness among many workers, in contrast with the deeply rooted corruption of people in power.

The Grapes of Wrath (1939) by John Steinbeck
- A hardworking but poor farm family loses its home to the banks during the Great Depression of the 1930s and then is driven from Oklahoma by the enduring drought resulting in the Dust Bowl. Eight members of the family board their one truck to drive to the promised land of California, only to find that there are few jobs paying even a little money for picking fruit. The meager work disappears at the season's end.

Worker exploitation is still alive today in the United States in commodity areas where migrant workers are employed. For many decades, migrant workers picking tomatoes in Florida would be harassed and bullied and given no rest breaks, although the temperature was 95 degrees in the sun. Crew leaders would often grope the women, demanding sex in exchange for steady jobs.[1]

Worker exploitation is found in many parts of the world. In 2012 the International Labor Organization (ILO) estimated that nearly 21 million individuals across the globe were living and working under conditions of quasi-slavery, including debt bondage, forced labor, child labor, human trafficking, and sex trafficking. The workers come to earn money but their cost of transport, rent, and food leaves them with very little as their debt increases and they lack the means to return home.[2]

Is labor exploitation an inherent feature of capitalism? If so, is it correctible by public policies to limit the hours of work and improve workers' safety, pay, and benefits? Or can it be corrected by joint action on the part of enlightened companies that won't use suppliers who abuse their workers? In an example of the latter situation, a consortium of companies including Wal-Mart, McDonald's, Yum Brands, Publix, and others formed the Coalition of Immokalee Workers, which refused to buy tomatoes from growers who were mistreating or underpaying their workers.

Working conditions are usually a function of whether workers are abundant or scarce. If workers are abundant, the company will post a low wage. If workers are scarce, the company will pay at a higher level. Yet in both cases, the pay level would hardly approach a *living wage*.

ORGANIZING UNIONS

When workers became highly aggrieved about their low wages and poor working conditions, they tried to organize trade or craft unions. Companies typically fought unions and the idea of collective bargaining on the grounds that workers were free to quit whenever they wanted and that unions violated the private property rights of owners. Although companies preferred no unions, some agreed to "open shop" unions where workers were not forced to join and pay membership fees. Unions tried to insist on "closed shop" unions that require all workers to pay dues, because this gives the union more money and manpower to fight management and go on strike if necessary. The closed shop also prevents "free riders," workers who benefit from a union without paying dues.

In the early days of the union movement, there were bitter strikes during which several companies hired thugs to break up the crowd of picketing workers. The Pullman Strike that started on May 11, 1894, showed the bitterness that could take place in labor-management relations. The Pullman Company made railway cars. When demand fell, the Pullman Company laid off many workers and cut wages for those who kept their jobs, but did not cut rents in the Pullman community where many workers lived. Nearly 4,000 factory employees began a wildcat strike that ultimately affected 250,000 workers in twenty-seven states. Riots and sabotage caused $80 million in damages and thirty people were killed. The workers in many industries felt exploited and launched frequent and often long-lasting strikes that were costly to both labor and management and the country at large.

Strikes were the union's great weapon. The United States passed laws entitling labor unions to strike and have the rights of collective bargaining. The unions fought for a "living wage" and decent benefits, including vacations, health benefits, and higher pay for overtime. Unions also pressed legislators to pass a minimum wage law. In 1955, they pressed for a minimum wage of $1 an hour. Business interests thought this rate was outrageous and would destroy the economy. The unions eventually succeeded in this goal, even though the minimum wage rarely amounted to a living wage.

THE QUESTION OF MINIMUM WAGES

Today the federal minimum wage is $7.25 an hour and has been in place since 2009. This minimum wage is substantially below a living wage! A person earning $7.25 an hour working forty hours a week would not be able to afford the average one-bedroom apartment in any single county within the United States. In Seattle, such an apartment would require a minimum wage of $17.56 and in San Mateo County, California, it would take $29.83.[3] Clearly the minimum wage of $7.25 an hour is woefully inadequate.

MIT prepared a living wage calculator to understand the gaps between what Americans earn and what they *need to earn* to cover basic needs. The living wage is not about a middle-class lifestyle and covers only the bare-bones cost of housing, food, transportation, and child and health care. In 2013, the living wage was $24.84 an hour in Massachusetts and $16.88 in Mississippi. These living-wage levels are far above today's minimum wage of $7.25 and remain substantially above even the proposed new minimum wage level of $10.10.[4]

Let's review what took place with workers' incomes since the late 1940s. From 1940 to 1980, American workers enjoyed a substantial increase in their incomes and quality of life, certainly in contrast to the Great Depression years before World War II. During this period, the great American middle class was built. The high level of prosperity began to decline in the 1980s. It has continued to fall for the next thirty-five years until today, leaving a much smaller middle class.

During the period 1990–2000, the top one percent of earners increased their share of the national income from 14 percent to 22 percent (an increase of 50 percent), while the remaining 99 percent of earners saw their share of national income drop from 86 percent to 78 percent (a decline of 10 percent). Given that 70 percent of our national income comes from consumer spending, this drop in the mass spending power of the middle class slowed down the growth of national income.

During the period 2000–2006, the Federal Reserve System under Alan Greenspan adopted a laissez-faire attitude that prevented any government regulation on the use of financial derivatives and led to the complete repeal of the Glass-Steagall Act, leaving the financial community unregulated. This and other factors set the conditions leading to the Great Recession of 2007–2011, which further impoverished many workers, who also lost their homes.[5]

What's Happening Today?

Workers are now organizing to raise the minimum wage of $7.25 to a significantly higher level. For example, fast-food workers are pushing for a $15 minimum wage—more than double the current figure. Senate Democrats want to raise the minimum to $10.10 over a three-year period. In 2013, Washington, D.C., passed a bill to require Wal-Mart to pay its workers a minimum "living wage" of $12.50 an hour for the privilege of opening six Wal-Mart stores there. Wal-Mart, which had fought hard for the right to open the stores in Washington, then threatened to reconsider entering the D.C. area.

Henry Ford in the 1920s was in favor of raising wages. He doubled workers' pay not because he was an altruist, but because his workforce suffered from high turnover and absenteeism and he felt that his workers had to earn enough to buy his cars.[6] Capitalists too often fail to see the connection between workers' low pay and the absence of strong demand for their products, but nobody can deny Henry Ford's credentials as a capitalist.

Some Republicans today are beginning to support an increase in the minimum wage. A conservative Republican, multimillionaire Ron Unz, is pushing in California for a referendum on a two-step minimum wage hike, first to $10 an hour in 2015 and then to $12 an hour in 2016. He wants to put an end to what he calls "poverty wages." His reasoning is very straightforward. He argues that companies, by not paying higher wages to workers, are shifting the burden to the taxpayers, who have to supply food stamps and other subsidies to help workers get by. He estimates that taxpayers paid a quarter-billion dollars every year from 2007 to 2011 for public assistance. If business would pay its fair share, he argues, taxpayers would save a trillion dollars in five years. Furthermore, the increase in their wages would mostly be spent and would boost California's economy, and the price increases by business would be minimal.[7]

The city of Seattle has passed a $15 minimum wage that would result in a 61 percent wage increase over its current minimum wage of $9.32.[8] Portland, Oregon, has also passed a $15 minimum wage. Those against these hikes include not only restaurateurs and other service providers, but even nonprofit groups that think such increases would produce too much unemployment, especially among immigrants and the poorest workers. They favor a more modest increase along the lines of President Obama's call for $10.10. I agree that minimum wages should be increased, but it should be done in a timed sequence of more moderate increases.

The reason for all this pressure is that neither $7.25, $10.10, $12.50, nor even $15.00 an hour provides a living wage. Low-wage workers, especially those working at fast-food outlets like McDonald's, mainly used to be teenagers or women looking for part-time work to supplement family income. Today, many of these workers are older and better educated and depend for their entire income on these low-paying jobs. The low pay is woefully inadequate. The order-takers you meet at McDonald's or the sales checkout people at Wal-Mart are the working poor. Many of them depend on food stamps and on Medicaid if they can get it.

The movement for a minimum wage was initially targeted at stopping sweatshop labor. Today, over 90 percent of the world's countries have minimum wage laws. Minimum wage rates vary greatly across many different jurisdictions, not only in prescribing a certain wage but also in treating special situations such as tipped income. If the U.S. minimum wage had kept pace with the average growth in productivity, it today would be about $17 an hour. But productivity gains have mainly flowed to profits, shareholders, and executives instead of workers. This fact contradicts Milton Friedman's famous statement that capitalism distributes the fruits of economic progress among all people. It is not true that all boats rise with rising productivity.

Disagreements About Raising the Minimum Wage

Among those who oppose raising the minimum wage are large companies such as Wal-Mart, McDonald's, and many restaurants that are paying the minimum wage of $7.25 or slightly more. These companies argue that workers would ultimately lose if the government established "too high" a minimum wage.[9] Companies would not only hire fewer workers but also would try to replace labor with machinery. This is exactly what happened in factories where an increasing amount of production is now done by automation and robot machines. The intended plan for the future supermarket is to collect cash without needing cashiers.

Businesses say that they will hire fewer workers if the minimum wage is raised. Existing workers would make more money, but those not hired would be worse off. Businesses complain that they will have to raise the wages of the more skilled workers as well, called the "ripple effect." Businesses warn that they will also have to raise their prices in order to recover the cost, in which case higher minimum wages will hurt families who have to pay more for their goods. This might be the case with fast-food retailers, where the margins are razor thin and where they would have to raise prices to cover the higher minimum wage. Small retail businesses such as restaurants warn that they might have to close if the minimum wage is raised. Manufacturers complain that raising the minimum wage will lead them to leave for cheaper labor countries and depress jobs here.

Until the mid-1990s, a strong consensus existed among economists, both conservative and liberal, that increasing the minimum wage would probably reduce employment, especially among younger and low-skill workers. Some people have proposed setting a sub-minimum wage for teenage workers so that they can get work experience, but this would lead to teens being hired instead of older unskilled workers.

Setting the actual minimum wage is a balancing act, trying to minimize the loss of jobs while preserving the country's international competitiveness. Many factors need to be considered, including the state of the economy, inflation potential, the prevailing average wage, level of unemployment, and the rate of productivity growth.

Unions argue that the minimum wage is particularly needed (1) when employers collude to keep the wages down; (2) where there is low job mobility, such as in company towns or where workers are loath to leave their homes and friends; and (3) where there is imperfect market information about where higher-paying jobs might be found.

There are many different empirical studies of the impact of minimum wage on employment with very different findings. The debate goes on not only between businesses and unions, but even within the economic profession. In 2013, economists were surveyed on their view of the minimum wage's impact on employment. About 34 percent of respondents agreed with the statement, "Raising the federal minimum wage to $9 per hour would make it noticeably harder for low-skilled workers to find employment," while 32 percent disagreed, and the remaining respondents were uncertain or had no opinion on the question.[10]

Economist Paul Krugman asserts there is hard evidence showing states that raised the minimum wage on their own haven't lost out in employment compared to neighboring states that didn't raise the minimum wage. Timothy Egan reports that "studies of nine cities and twenty-one states that upped their minimum over the last decade found almost no effect on employment. Businesses had less turnover and higher worker productivity, while restaurant prices went up only 2 or 3 percent."[11]

If there are few adverse effects on employment, wouldn't it be better to raise the minimum wage nationally? The Economic Policy Institute estimated that an increase in the national minimum wage to $10.10 from its current $7.25 would benefit 30 million workers. And when you consider that those benefiting are likely to spend all the extra income, the increase could have an acceleration impact on income and employment.[12]

ALTERNATIVE PROPOSALS TO HELP WORKERS GET A LIVING WAGE

Some economists and political commentators have proposed alternative remedies to help unskilled workers improve their income. These remedies would benefit a broader population of low-wage earners and distribute the costs more widely, rather than putting all the burden on the heavy employers of low-wage workers. Proposals include establishing higher taxes on the rich, increasing the ease of forming unions, and establishing more government job creation and job training programs.

One provocative proposal is to establish a *basic income* that provides each citizen with a sum of money that is sufficient to live on. Sometimes this is called a "negative income tax." It is a transfer payment from the government that comes from the broad tax base and doesn't impose any loss of efficiency on different business groups.[13] The argument is that unemployed people are more expensive to maintain than keeping them employed. If they are unemployed, they will receive unemployment insurance, food stamps, and welfare services that would cost more than the government paying them to work on useful projects. There are so many useful work projects—fixing the country's infrastructure, caring for the aged, teaching literacy, and so on—that putting Americans to work through publicly financed jobs would be good for the unemployed and good for the country.

A *guaranteed minimum income* is a variant that is conditioned on a means test and the person's willingness to participate in the private-sector labor market or perform community services. Several arguments have been advanced in favor of the government providing every citizen with a minimum income. First, no one would go hungry. Second, people could leave a hated job and start their own business. Third, the government could eliminate the inefficient patchwork of current programs (e.g., welfare, food stamps, housing vouchers, and others) in favor of a simpler system that in a single stroke does the job of delivering a minimum income to everyone.[14]

Another approach is called a *refundable tax credit,* available only to households that have earned some income, where the government can reduce the tax owed to zero and add net payment to the taxpayer. [15]

A quite different approach (used in Germany, Italy, Sweden, and Denmark) is called *co-determination,* which lets the minimum wage be set by collective bargaining in the company or industry. There is no minimum wage set by government.[16]

A stronger proposal than co-determination is to favor establishing more *Workers' Self-Directed Enterprises* (WSDEs). Here, workers own shares in the company, called an ESOP (Employee Stock Ownership Plan). They participate in running the company and in deciding what is produced, how it is produced, where it is produced, and how profits are to be used and distributed. Normally these business decisions are made by an owner or investors with less consideration of their impact on the workers.

Some have suggested getting more workers to own stock in their own company or other companies, thereby turning them into capitalists who might have influence on corporate policies. However, this outcome likely would be a long time in coming because today one percent of U.S. shareholders own 75 percent of the outstanding stock. Furthermore, most workers don't have spare money to invest in stocks or bonds. They are more likely to put any surplus money into home ownership instead of stocks or bonds.

Then there are calls for establishing a *universal savings plan* for retirement in addition to Social Security. Workers and their employers have been contributing to Social Security so that the workers receive payments upon retiring. But in the future, Social Security income may not be adequate. Some percentage of workers independently decided to build their own private retirement accounts in addition to Social Security. On average, the median couple in the United States carries a private retirement account averaging $42,000. Those favoring a universal savings plan call for companies to contribute 50-cents-per-hour for each employee in a portable plan managed by a privately run, low-fee, life-cycle fund. The money would be invested in an appropriate mix of stocks and bonds. In this sense, the workers would become capitalists to some degree! It's estimated that a person beginning work at age 22 with such a plan would retire at age 67 with a balance of $160,000, substantially more than the current $42,000 average balance. This would handsomely supplement workers' Social Security receipts and enable them to live better upon retirement.[17]

THE ISSUE OF WORKER SATISFACTION ON THE JOB

Even if workers received a living wage, many would still be dissatisfied with their jobs. Such would be the case with jobs that are hard, such as construction work; jobs that are dangerous, such as mining; and jobs that are boring, such as cashiering or "shelving" in a supermarket or putting a walnut on each piece of chocolate coming down the production line. Even in the professions, such as law and teaching, there is much boring work. The challenge facing companies is whether they can do anything to make work more interesting and "happify" their employees. Everyone has had the experience of shopping in a big-box store such as Wal-Mart or a fast-food chain like McDonald's and seeing them staffed with many unhappy and unhelpful people. These organizations view workers largely as a cost that must be contained. Ikea manages its 130,000 global workers using workforce management software to assign and train them in the most efficient way to keep costs down. Yet customers might experience too few people on the floor to answer questions or willing to go out of their way to help the customer.

The view is growing, however, that companies would be more profitable if they would pay their employees more and treat them better. Employees who have more job satisfaction would engage with the customers to find out what they really want. They might even be empowered to show off merchandise and improve displays and would end up selling more goods and services, which would feed back into more employee job satisfaction. Companies such as Costco, Trader Joe's, Nordstrom, Zappos, Lego, and others have higher employee satisfaction and outperform their competitors even though they pay more to their employees.

Consider Tony Hsieh, CEO of Zappos, whose organization is highly successful in selling shoes online. He wants Zappos to be a happy place for his employees. Other companies have studied his methods.[18] His consultancy, called "Delivering Happiness at Work," consists of a three-day boot camp to teach companies to become more successful through the science of happiness.

Paul Zak, a neuroscience researcher, has proposed that employees who have trust in their organization and see a higher purpose to their work will experience more joy (Trust × Purpose = Joy). His research team has found evidence that confirms happy employees are more productive, are more innovative, and contribute more to the bottom line of companies.[19] Similar findings have been reported by Zeynep Ton, an MIT business professor, who said that "contrary to conventional corporate thinking, treating retail workers much better may make everyone (including their employers) much richer."[20]

Some progressive companies go even further and want to invest in enhancing their employees' healthful living. In the United States, workplace wellness is a $6 billion industry. Companies offer programs to improve the health and well-being of their employees in the hope that it will increase their productivity, reduce their risk of costly chronic diseases, and improve their control of chronic conditions.[21] Company wellness programs have two parts: lifestyle management and disease management. The lifestyle management program tries to help employees eat healthier foods, give up smoking, and exercise regularly to avoid obesity, diabetes, cancer, hypertension, and other health problems. The disease management program helps employees with a chronic disease take better care of themselves by reminding them to take their prescribed medications and not miss lab tests or doctor's appointments. Many of these programs have yielded a better life to employees and a financially sound return to the companies.

One additional factor in job satisfaction is paid vacations and holidays. "All work and no play" is a prescription for disaster. A report about working hours in China carried the headline that Chinese workers are dying on the job from overwork.[22] Workers deserve and need vacation time to renew their energy and outlook. The United States is the only wealthy economy that does not require employers to provide paid vacation time or paid holidays.[23] One in four Americans do not receive any paid vacation or paid holidays. In contrast, most advanced countries provide both paid holidays in addition to paid vacation days. For example, the European Union legally guarantees workers at least twenty paid vacation days per year, and workers also get between five and thirteen paid holidays a year. The lack of paid vacation and paid holidays in the United States falls especially hard on low-wage workers, part-time workers, and employees of small businesses.

*   *   *

Under capitalism, businesses operate to make a profit that will yield a good return to the owners or investors. Businesses need to keep their costs down, especially their labor costs. If there is an oversupply of labor, businesses will take advantage by setting the lowest wages possible, whether or not they constitute a living wage. This leads workers in many cases to organize into unions to press for better pay and enlist government support to legislate a minimum wage. Businesses originally fought against these unions and blocked unions from organizing, sometimes even with police support and violence. But unions and collective bargaining began to prevail in many countries. Unfortunately, there is a suspicion on the part of some workers that unions have become self-serving and have not effectively raised workers' incomes. In the United States, unions are weak today, which raises the question of why so many workers in manufacturing and service industries refuse to unionize. One test of workers' willingness to unionize occurred in early 2014, with a workers' vote at a Volkswagen factory in Tennessee. The workers voted 712 to 626 against joining the United Auto Workers (UAW), marking another defeat for the union movement.

There is little doubt that the union movement helped workers earn higher wages and benefits and raise their standard of living. Worker exploitation is at a lower level today than in the past in most advanced economies. Raising minimum wages is one tool for increasing the pay of the most unskilled workers. Some economists have also talked about other alternatives such as a guaranteed minimum income, refundable tax credits, or co-determination solutions between management and labor.

FOUR

JOB CREATION IN THE FACE OF GROWING AUTOMATION

In many cases, jobs that used to be done by people are going to be able to be done through automation. I don't have an answer to that. That's one of the more perplexing problems of society.

— JOHN SCULLEY

We want to consider not only worker well-being today (see Chapter 3), but also what the outlook will be for worker well-being in the future, particularly whether capitalism can create enough jobs for people in a future marked by growing automation. The International Labor Organization, an agency of the United Nations, estimates that the number of unemployed worldwide is now over 200 million and is likely to get worse.[1]

Consider that in the 1870s, 70 to 80 percent of the U.S. population was employed in agriculture. Today, the part of the population employed in agriculture is less than 2 percent. Fortunately, manufacturing increased to supply enough jobs as agriculture declined. By 1973, manufacturing accounted for 22 percent of the American gross domestic product (GDP). But today manufacturing accounts for only 9 percent of the GDP. As agriculture and manufacturing go down, more jobs need to be created by the service industries. Can the service industries create enough jobs, and will there be enough decent-paying jobs?

THE IMPACT OF TECHNOLOGY

Early warnings about technology destroying jobs occurred during the Industrial Revolution in Britain. From 1811 to 1817, companies in the apparel industry kept introducing newly developed labor-saving machinery that threatened to replace artisans with less-skilled, low-wage workers, leaving them without work. Workers in Nottingham organized a protest movement. The protesters were called the Luddites, named after Ned Ludd, a young man who had earlier smashed two stocking frames in 1779. The Luddite movement spread throughout England, involving handloom weavers burning mills and destroying pieces of factory machinery and other groups destroying wool and cotton mills. The British government suppressed the movement by 1817. Meanwhile, skilled artisans formed friendly societies to help silk workers and weavers fight unemployment and oppose "foreign" labor entering into their trades.

Technology is clearly destroying many jobs, probably faster than it is creating new jobs. Technology has been a job killer and disrupter of several industries, including publishing, music, retail, and manufacturing. We may be losing the race against the machine. Geoff S. Jones, a forty-nine-year-old car factory worker, believes that reduced need for human workers will decrease the ability of consumers to buy products. He writes in *MIT Technology Review*:

> Those consequences will lead to some type of economic collapse if they're not corrected—the magnitude of change is beyond the abil-

ity of our government and financial institutions to survive. The corporate need for ever-increasing profit will accelerate the use of robotics. I believe this is inevitable and unstoppable. Sounds like a good plot for some hard-core science fiction.[2]

I remember reading a science fiction story many years ago about an economy that becomes so automated there is little work left for humans to do. Everything produced is available in abundance. In fact, the government requires citizens to consume more than they want in order to keep the manufacturing equipment going. A few jobs are still available, and citizens bid intensely for these few jobs. They come from a generation that grew up working, and they want to keep working because there is nothing else they know or want to do with their time.

How automatized can a factory become? The idea of the assembly line goes way back to Adam Smith saying that each worker should make only a part of the product, such as the pinhead instead of the whole pin. Workers would no longer be artisans making the whole product, but instead specialists in one repetitious act.

In the early 1900s, Frederick Winslow Taylor pioneered the development of "scientific management" to find methods to increase output and reduce labor. As labor productivity is increased, fewer workers are needed to produce a given level of output. Henry Ford applied many of Taylor's methods in developing efficient assembly lines in the manufacture of automobiles. According to Simon Head, in his book *Mindless: Why Smarter Machines Are Making Dumber Humans*, this amounts to "dumbing down" workers, turning them into robots who learn to do only one thing well or at least fast enough to get it done before the item moves ahead on the assembly line.[3]

Advances in technology allowed companies to build machines that could duplicate the work done by employees. The machines were increasingly driven by intelligent programs to perform repetitive tasks. Soon management began to visualize the whole factory being operated by one person who would watch the dials—plus one dog to make sure this person doesn't fall asleep.

This managerial drive to control output and reduce labor did not stop with the factory. As service industries grew, management developed "cognitive digital control systems" to increase or improve service outputs in service industries. Simon Head discusses how Cathay Pacific trained its air hostesses to smile more and how college professors in England are measured by key performance indicators (KPIs) based on "balanced scorecards" to judge whether they should be promoted. The point is, there is a drive to robotize human behavior to make it more predictable and efficient.

Can automation reduce the number of jobs in the retail sector? Definitely! This is already happening. Customers walking up to Jessops, a seventy-eight-year-old British camera store, saw an ironic sign plastered on the front door: THE STAFF AT JESSOPS WOULD LIKE TO THANK YOU FOR SHOPPING WITH AMAZON.

As more shopping moves over to digital sites like Amazon, many stores will close and join the ranks of the late Borders bookstores, Virgin Megastores (France), Comet white-goods and electronics stores (Britain), and Tower Records (America). The fact is that the prices of goods are often lower on digital sites, especially if no sales taxes are collected. Furthermore, digital sites are working hard to speed up delivery so that waiting won't discourage purchasing. Jeff Bezos bought a company called Kiva to do robotic sorting in warehouses and currently is investing in drones as a future delivery system, much to the consternation of the U.S. Postal Service and FedEx. Marc Andreessen, the digital venture capitalist, predicted, "Retail guys are going to go out of business and e-commerce will become the place everyone buys."[4] The question for us is, what will happen to all the people who worked in those stores? Certainly the digital sites will grow and hire more people, but far fewer than work in in-store retailing today.

FEWER JOBS FOR MORE PEOPLE

At the same time that automation is reducing the number of jobs, the labor supply is actually increasing. Many people who've lost their jobs are still out there looking for work—not all of them have given up the search. Legions of young people just out of college are struggling to find meaningful employment. As a result, there are more people looking for fewer jobs.

Let's add another disturbing thought about the job creation question. Will there be enough jobs if the United States reduces its military spending on equipment and supplies and fewer military personnel are needed? National security spending accounts for more than half of all federal discretionary spending. During 2008, Pentagon data reported that the federal government maintained 5,429 bases in the United States and thirty-eight foreign nations. If defense spending were cut in half, we would have to close most of the foreign military bases and reduce spending on weapons development. This will represent the loss of a great number of military-related jobs. Add the fact that many veterans will return as we reduce our boots-on-the-ground military commitments in Iraq and Afghanistan. Where will the new jobs for all of these people come from?

Has the high level of military spending and our engagement in a number of wars been largely about job creation? We built 32,000 nuclear bombs (8,500 still exist), while only a few would have been enough to deter aggressors. The United States is building supercarriers for $12 billion each (a total of $120 billion) and F-35 combat jets for $80 million each (a total of $325 billion) at a time when most fighting against terrorists is carried out door-to-door or by drones. What is the connection between capitalism and militarism?[5]

Another development may further increase the supply of labor. American prisons today are swelling with inmates. The number of prisoners increased from 300,000 in 1970 to about 2 million in 2000. The

United States accounts for 25 percent of the world's prison population. Many inmates are incarcerated for drug charges. The War on Drugs hasn't been successful; in fact, it's been a disaster. Now, with more liberal treatment accorded to drug cases, many prisoners will receive reduced sentences and earlier release. Can good jobs be made available to them? Employers will run background checks, and many of them may not be willing to hire ex-prisoners. With the scarcity of jobs, ex-offenders will find it especially difficult to get work.[6]

The specter of a diminishing number of jobs has come up a number of times, especially during each of the many recessions when people were let go because of falling demand. This was such a serious question during the Great Depression of the 1930s that the U.S. government went into deep deficit spending to create jobs, guided by the theory of the economist John Maynard Keynes, who said that jobs can be created by fiscal policy even if monetary policy didn't work. Employment slowly rose in the construction and other industries until 1937, when the government reduced its stimulus. Unemployment didn't seriously go down until the country started to prepare for possible participation in World War II.

The good news is that all past business cycles eventually ended and jobs reappeared. The real question is whether the rapid acceleration of automation and information technology will put a new face on the problem of job creation. Jeremy Rifkin addressed this problem in his 1995 book *The End of Work*.[7] Rifkin pointed to the rapid increase in the use of automation and information technology as potentially eliminating millions of jobs in the manufacturing, agriculture, retail, and service industries. He contended that the incomes of knowledge workers who produce the automation and information would increase, but not enough new jobs would be created to equal the number of old jobs destroyed. Even if they did, low-skilled workers would have lost their jobs and gone on welfare. Rifkin saw the possibility of worldwide unemployment leading to the need for more government welfare in the form of a "social wage" and the growth of the third sector of not-for-profit organizations to supplement the government's provision of needed social services.

WHO WILL BE AFFECTED MOST?

There is a debate about which groups will be most affected by technological advances in automation. One would think low-skilled workers would be hurt the most because machines can be built to do unskilled routine work. But it can be countered that these machines may cost more than simply paying low wages to low-skilled workers. It may be that white-collar and middle-management workers will lose out to intelligent machines in areas such as accounting, financial analysis, and programming. Much bookkeeping is now done by automation. Many people can prepare their own legal service documents without using lawyers. The advent of 3-D printing makes it possible to replace some skilled artisans who do forging and welding. We may not need as many high school and college professors since students can learn much on their own by watching videos from massive open online course (MOOC) libraries describing many business theories and practices. The medical industry produces videos with avatars that can guide patients on rehabilitation exercises while watching a TV screen, reducing the need for health care facilities to have as many trained rehabilitation specialists.

There is no doubt that automation is impacting skilled and professional workers. An Oxford University study estimated that 47 percent of today's jobs could be automated in the next two decades. The book *The Second Machine Age* shows how the field of "cognitive computing" is advancing in its use of "natural" language to undertake many complex tasks. IBM's Watson has shown how machines can answer questions faster and recommend better answers and treatments for medical issues.

One critical question is whether there are brainier jobs that cannot be done by machines, and enough of these jobs. The other question is whether new types of work can be invented at a faster pace to replace the jobs that are being lost.[8] New businesses tend to employ far fewer workers than in the past. Instagram, the photo-sharing site, was bought by Facebook for $1 billion in 2012 and had 30 million customers managed by thirteen people, whereas Kodak, a victim of the digital revolution, had to file for bankruptcy after once employing 145,000 people in its heyday.

Unemployment might rise even higher if the gap keeps increasing between the incomes of the rich and the poor. In the last thirty years, labor's share of output has shrunk globally from 64 percent to 59 percent. Meanwhile, the income share going to the top one percent in America has risen from around 9 percent in the 1970s to 22 percent today. With fewer dollars in the hands of most Americans, they won't be buying as many cars, television sets, kitchen appliances, and other items to constitute sufficient demand that therefore could create more jobs. Even then, many of these goods are imported and end up increasing the number of jobs in other countries rather than in the United States. Will the U.S. middle class get smaller and be replaced by a hyper-unequal economy that's run by the top one percent of capital-owners and "super-managers"?[9]

SLOWER ECONOMIC GROWTH?

The underlying uncertainty about jobs is whether the U.S. economic outlook suggests slow growth or fast growth. I've already hinted that the outlook is for slow growth. This view has been promulgated by the economist Robert J. Gordon of Northwestern University in his paper "Is U.S. Economic Growth Over?: Faltering Innovation Confronts the Six Headwinds."[10] (One writer described this article as the most depressing economic idea of 2012.)

Gordon believes the big gains in productivity that supported an expanding middle class and the modern welfare state won't be repeated in the future. He sees technology continuing to grow, but not likely to bring about brand-new breakthroughs on the scale of the steam engine, the internal combustion engine, indoor plumbing, electricity, the railroad, automobiles, airplanes, computers, and the Internet. Each of these inventions created spin-offs, such as highways, air-conditioning, and efficient factories that kept the economy growing for decades more. Gordon admits that the Internet and the digital revolution still has plenty of growth potential left, but he doesn't expect it to have an impact on the scale of previous major innovations.

Furthermore, Gordon sees six other forces in the economy that are likely to dampen U.S. growth: "our aging population, our faltering education system, growing income inequality, rising foreign competition, the inevitable impact of global warming, and the need to eventually pay down our debt." From 1891 to 2007, the nation achieved a robust 2 percent annual growth rate of output per person. Gordon estimates that these six forces will cut down half of the annual GDP income per capita to one percent growth. And he thinks innovation will be less than what produced our annual growth in the past. Put together, he thinks that our economy will at best grow at 0.5 percent per year for the next few decades. He suggests that the rapid growth made over the past 250 years could well turn out to be a unique episode in human history. He sees these forces combining to spell stagnation and a future decline in living standards.

ACQUIRING NEW SKILLS

There are, ironically, many skilled and middle-class jobs that can't find workers. In August 2013, U.S. companies were unable to fill 7 million jobs, mostly in the science, technology, engineering, and mathematics (STEM) fields.[11] There is a disconnect between the skills that workers have or are acquiring and the skills that are actually needed. Low-skill jobs are being decimated by technology, creating a major unemployment problem. And not enough students are studying STEM subjects to equip them for a large choice of jobs when they graduate.

Clearly the demand for STEM skills is terribly out of balance with the present and future workforce skills, not only in the United States, but also in China and India and emerging countries. What are the possible solutions?

1. Set up better job-retraining programs for the current workforce, focusing on the types of jobs that will be in chronic short supply.

2. Do a better job of training U.S. students in math and science at the elementary and high school levels. Less than 10 percent of American students scored at the highest level of math, whereas in such countries as Switzerland, Finland, Japan, South Korea, and Belgium, 20 percent of students can perform at the highest math level. The need is to develop better educational leaders and better classroom teachers. This will require improving the salaries and status of teachers in our society to the level found in the most educationally competitive countries.

3. Educate high school students to better understand the job market so that they can make wiser career choices.

4. Bring together educators, businesses, and government groups, at the local level, to develop a shared vision of how to improve their job pipeline.

5. Encourage businesses to invest more in human capital development and be able to depreciate the cost of their investment, the same as they do with physical equipment.

6. Make it easier to attract more foreign talent to come and work in the country. Reduce the present impediments that limit entry visas.

ENCOURAGING ENTREPRENEURSHIP

Are there potential developments that could get the country back to a 2 percent GDP annual growth rate and create the necessary jobs? One approach is to encourage and facilitate a strong interest in and support of entrepreneurship. There are still many needs that go unsatisfied and there are many people with good ideas on how to satisfy these needs. These entrepreneurs need capital and knowledgeable help to create their businesses. Fortunately, the U.S. harbors many venture capital firms and there are many financial "angels" who might advance funds to would-be entrepreneurs.[12]

However, entrepreneurs face many hurdles in starting a business beyond their need for funding. How easy is it to start a new business in any country? Countries vary greatly in this respect. New Zealand is rated as the easiest place in the world to create a new business. Starting a business requires "one procedure, half a day, (and) less than one percent of income per capita and no paid-in minimum capital." The top five countries in the ease of starting a new business include New Zealand, Canada, Singapore, Australia, and Hong Kong. The United States, by contrast, ranks well behind countries like Rwanda, Belarus, and Azerbaijan in terms of the ease of starting a new business. It requires an average of six procedures, five days, and 1.5 percent of the company's income per capita when starting a new U.S. business.[13]

Nobody can predict the extent of new job creation through entrepreneurship and other means. Here are some possibilities that I would point to:

- There are many new technologies that have promising futures. Among them are mobile Internet, automation of knowledge work, Internet of Things (smart sensor technologies), cloud technology, advanced robotics, autonomous and near-autonomous vehicles, next-generation genomics, energy storage, 3-D printing, advanced materials, advanced oil and gas exploration and recovery, and renewable energy. Although none of these may singly produce the next great innovation, cumulatively their future impact can be great.

• Many manufacturing jobs might start coming back to the United States as foreign costs increase and as more value is placed on quick turnarounds. Although many products, such as those from Apple, are produced abroad, many of the designers and engineers and distribution experts are in the U.S. They are factoryless goods producers who should be but are not included in the manufacturing section of GDP.

• Technology replaces some existing jobs, but also creates new jobs. It also can lead money to flow into other hands through lower prices, higher wages, or higher profits, all of which stimulates demand that can possibly lead to hiring more workers. Corporate America is sitting on $2 trillion of cash in bank accounts abroad. Corporations don't want to bring the cash back to the United States because the U.S. corporate tax rate is 35 percent (the average in other countries is about 20 percent). If this tax rate could be lowered, money would pour into the U.S. to build needed factories and infrastructure, which would greatly boost employment. The new GDP generated would well make up for the lost tax revenue resulting from the lower tax rate.

SUPPORTING THE UNEMPLOYED

If job creation remains low, what can be done to assist the unemployed? We already know that certain groups are particularly unable to find jobs. The unemployment rate is high for young African Americans. College students are graduating with accumulated student debt of over $1 trillion. And many seniors who lose their jobs are finding it hard to be rehired or find work at the wages they formerly received. How are these people to be supported?

Sadly, the cost of supporting the unemployed exceeds the cost of creating a job for them. This suggests that the great needs of the society for better education, health, and infrastructure ought to be met by the government supplying these jobs in the absence of the private sector creating them. The private sector's interest lies in reducing its payroll expenses, not creating new jobs. As the government's role increases in supplying work for the unemployed, it must fund the programs (much like the Works Progress Administration and the Civilian Conservation Corps in the 1930s) through either higher taxes or printing more money. The former becomes harder because of citizen resistance to higher taxes in an economy with more poor people. The alternative, printing money, has the potential of producing runaway inflation.

Among the better proposals for supporting the unemployed are the following:

- Share the work. Reduce the average workweek to thirty-five hours, as France did in February 2000. Assuming that the same amount of work remains to be done, the assumption is that companies will need to hire more workers. This did not happen in France, however, largely because French companies find it hard to lay off workers and don't want to be stuck with more workers. France simply found ways to get more output from the existing workers.
- Establish a three-day workweek of eleven hours a day. Workers would have more time for family and they will constitute a larger market for entertainment and self-development products and services. This idea was proposed by the world's second richest man, Carlos Slim of Mexico; it was also proposed, in some form, by Larry Page of Google.[14]
- Offer longer unpaid vacations. Honeywell did this.

- Increase the programs in job training and retraining. Recall that there are some industries—computer programming, certain engineering areas, the Internet—that might have worker shortages. Some U.S. industries are in short supply of certain technical skills and are anxious to import skilled people for these jobs. The DeVry Education Group and others offer many programs to train people in needed skills.

- Undertake a vigorous program to rebuild our deteriorating infrastructure—bridges, ports, airports, water and sewage systems—and build solar and wind farms and better electric grids.

- Establish "social wages" for those who have tried to get jobs but have not been successful. They will have more money to spend on goods and services, which will increase the number of jobs.

- Help American companies increase their exports from their U.S.-based businesses.

- Attract more foreign companies to locate their factories and offices in the United States to increase the number of jobs.

*   *   *

There are signs arising of a permanent class of long-term unemployed persons. Some persons make this their choice because they can't get the kind of jobs they want. Others decide that they can make enough income working part-time or in temporary service jobs and then applying for unemployment insurance and food stamps, which allows them to make more than they would working at a $7.25 minimum wage. Some people can live on their inheritances or live at home with their family. Certainly, we need to examine the different groups that make up the long-term unemployed and see if they can be brought back to favor full-time jobs.

The kinds of jobs that are increasing in the United States are mostly in retail sales and fast food, temporary work (with no benefits), and low-paying service jobs. What does this mean for students who borrow great sums of money to get a college education with the prospect of ending up flipping hamburgers or being a greeter at Wal-Mart?

A person's life meaning and dignity are highly connected to having a job and being able to move to a better job. When farmers left the land, they found plentiful jobs in industry. They didn't need much of an education. Now industry has largely moved overseas. Today's workers have to find jobs in the service trades. But many services require specific skills and people with low education often won't qualify. The society has clearly lost its previous high mobility. The question is whether we can get back to a job-abundant society.

FIVE

COMPANIES NOT COVERING THEIR "SOCIAL COSTS"

The only way you may correct the bad things in your past is to add better things to your future.

—SHILOH MORRISON

Capitalism works best when there is perfect information and perfect mobility characterizing all of the market participants. A producer would know the costs of producing in different places and be free to move production to lower-cost areas. And consumers would know where the best-paying jobs are and be able to move to the best-paying jobs.

But information and mobility are far from perfect. Each producer and consumer has to bear the cost of information search and mobility. A move to another location for production or consumption would pay as long as the gross improvement in the producer's or the consumer's situation is larger than the costs borne for better information and better mobility.

One role of government is to help improve the business information available to producers, middlemen, and consumers. Governments carry out information censuses and samples about almost every industry, company, and product. Today, the Internet makes access to business knowledge quick and easy for both businesses and individuals.

Economists have worked on the theory of what makes an economy perfectly efficient. The economy is said to reach a "Pareto optimum" if no voluntary exchange of labor or capital or allocation of goods and services will make some people better off and other people worse off. *Market failures* exist when some market participants can be made better off without making others worse off.

Here are three types of market failure that can occur under capitalism. They are:

1. Businesses and consumers ignoring costs they cause for which they are not charged, which is called the problem of *negative externalities*
2. Public goods that are abused if not regulated or rationed, which is called the *tragedy of the commons*
3. Monopolistic or oligopolistic control of industries and markets, which is called the *monopoly* problem

COMPANIES AVOIDING SOCIAL COSTS

You might expect that a company involved in production would bear all the costs resulting from its activity. A steel company would pay for the iron ore, the electricity, equipment depreciation, employees' wages, and so on. However, it is less likely that the steel company would be charged for the air pollution it caused or the water pollution from its chemicals that might have floated into the river. Air and water pollution are social costs that someone else may have to cover, either citizens who suffer from pollution or the government that might have to clean up the pollution and cover the health costs of victims.

The main point here is to identify the spillover effects of economic activity or processes that affect those who are not directly involved. Odors from a chemical factory can have negative spillover effects on the factory's neighbors.

Total cost consists of private cost and social cost. The social cost is a "negative externality" in the production of steel. If the steel company was required to pay for this cost, it would have to raise its prices or be left with less money and produce less steel. By avoiding their social costs, companies price lower than they should and end up producing more output. Someone else has to pay for the pollution.

Because governments now have less money available to clean up pollution, it would be better to charge businesses for the pollution caused by their production arrangements. A charge would give each business an incentive to search for ways to reduce its level of carbon emission.

Two systems have been proposed. One is to put a tax on carbon emissions because carbon releases greenhouse gases into the atmosphere. Harvard economist Dale Jorgenson and his coauthors favor putting a tax on carbon.[1] The higher a company's carbon emissions, the higher its tax bill. This will cause companies to reduce their carbon emissions.

Others have proposed a system that sets a limit on emissions, which is lowered over time if emissions decline. Each company estimates its carbon emission and needs to buy carbon credits. Suppose a business emits 100 tons of carbon each year and is required to buy enough carbon credits to cover 100 tons. The business later decides to buy pollution control equipment or switch from coal to lower pollution energy sources and manages to reduce its carbon emissions to 50 tons a year. Now it needs to buy only half as many carbon credits. If it had purchased carbon credits for 100 tons but now needs only 50, it can sell the 50 surplus carbon credits either to another business that needs them to cover its polluting costs, or on a spot market at the market price. Such a system is called a *cap-and-trade system*. The government puts a cap on how much pollution can be tolerated, and companies can buy and sell carbon credits to cover the cost of the pollution they emit. Their carbon credit costs will lead them to search for ways to reduce their emissions. Through emission trading, companies will be acting more responsibly about air pollution.

The question is how fast should the cap level be reduced? Many have favored lowering the cap at a rate to limit the earth's temperature from rising more than two degrees Centigrade. But this rate is not universally accepted, and some countries may not join in this cap-and-trade system. One suggestion is to put "carbon tariffs" on imported goods coming from nonparticipating countries, an idea disliked by the World Trade Organization. The question is, do we prefer to save the planet or continue to practice "free trade"?

As for controlling water pollution, the government would state what can and cannot be dropped into water and set penalties for such pollution. If the penalties are sufficiently high, the polluter would need to find some other way to dispose of bad chemicals.

Negative externalities also occur on the consumption side, not just the production side. The behavior of consumers can create negative externalities. Smokers pass on toxic harm to nonsmokers in the same room. People who litter on streets and in parks are imposing a cleanup cost on society. Car owners who buy high-pollution cars or do a lot of driving add to the pollution level. Consumers who prefer products that come from distant lands cause extra pollution because of all the extra fuel consumed in long-distance transportation.

In these cases, the government can pass laws to reduce some of these negative externalities. Government usually charges a higher registration license on cars that emit more pollution. Government places a high tax on cigarettes and encourages nonsmoking signs in offices and public transportation to protect citizens from the harmful effects of secondary smoke.

It must be recognized that producers and consumers can also generate positive externalities. A company that spends money on training its employees creates a benefit that goes beyond the benefit to itself in that the workers are more educated. One can imagine a case where a company claims to have created a set of positive benefits and proposes that they offset the negative externalities. Wal-Mart could claim that its ability to offer consumers low prices and its employees training offsets the argument against the low wages it pays.

Negative externalities are found in systems other than capitalism. Fortunately, capitalism has found a way to handle them using the market system itself to reduce or lower these negative externalities.

PROTECTING PUBLIC GOODS

I've discussed how owners of private goods may have to cover social costs connected with the use of these goods. Now let's turn to public goods that are owned and valued by the public. I'm thinking of parks, rivers, lakes, and forests. I believe it's necessary for government to put limits on the use of public goods to protect their quality.

A standard illustration is the grazing land for sheep. Suppose there are two sheep owners, and each lets his sheep graze on his land. Suppose there is another stretch of land that is public land located between the two sheep owners' properties. A sheep owner would be better off using the public land for grazing than his own land. Both sheep owners would see this as an opportunity and bring their sheep to graze on the public land first. The result would be overgrazing, and soon the public land would not grow enough grass for grazing. Only then would the two sheep owners bring their sheep to graze on their own private land.

The same problem would happen with forests or the sea if they are not protected. Too much timber would be cut or overfishing would lead to the disappearance of certain fish.

To prevent the tragedy of the commons, two solutions are available. One is to issue a set of rules for citizens who want to make use of the public good. A public park might issue rules: It is open only from 9 a.m. to 6 p.m.; dogs are not allowed to relieve themselves unless the owner carries a poop bag; littering is prohibited and punishable by a fine; no campfires are permitted.

The other solution is issuing permits to prevent the overuse of a public good. The government decides on how much use can be made of a public good and issues hunting and fishing permits. Some national parks that are overcrowded limit the number of visitors per day.

Many places in the world need to limit the use of water where water is scarce. India uses half of the world's water and doesn't use it efficiently. It could learn the drip method in agriculture used in Israel, also short of water, which is ten times more efficient. Governments can consider a number of measures. The price of water can be raised. People can be encouraged to shower or bathe less often and to water their lawns less often. The government can issue caps on industry and farmers' use of water. The government can prevent oil and gas hydraulic fracturing (or fracking, for short), which uses an excessive amount of water.

MONOPOLIES AND BARRIERS TO ENTRY

The purpose of a capitalist economy is to rely on open and free competition to set prices and outputs. If one company or industry is earning high profits, other companies need to be free to compete by offering lower prices or better products. Healthy competition keeps market prices and profits from becoming excessive. This assumes that there are no barriers to entry.

The fact is that many barriers can exist to prevent a competitor from entering an attractive market. Such barriers protect incumbent firms and restrict competition in a market. They represent a cost of entry that the new firm must bear, but not the firms already existing in the industry. They prevent a socially beneficial result from happening that would increase output and lower price.

Among the most prominent barriers to entry are:

- *Legal Barriers.* Zoning laws or transport agreements can prevent entry; other examples are protective tariffs on imports; switching barriers, such as long-term contracts making it expensive to change to a new competitor; the lack of essential resources needed for production; and the ownership of patents that prevent the entering firm from gaining access to necessary technology.

- *Cost Barriers.* They include the high cost of required advertising to establish the new brand; the high cost of required capital; the high cost of attracting distributors and suppliers when there are exclusive agreements; the low possibility of achieving scale to bring down cost to the level enjoyed by the present industry leaders; the high cost of obtaining the necessary licenses and permits; the high cost of dealing with predatory pricing by the dominant firm to stop entry; and the high cost of research and development (R&D).

All of these factors perpetuate the dominant firms' leadership in the market. The leading firms work hard to prevent the entry of new firms or the rise of existing minor firms. The leaders develop a strong brand and loyal customers who are willing to pay more.

The extreme anticompetitive case is where a monopoly exists—namely, one seller of an important good or service where near substitutes don't exist. Sometime this may be a *natural monopoly*, where a firm's per-unit cost decreases as it increases output and where one firm is most efficient from a cost perspective. Here the government may decide that it would be inefficient to have more than one firm supply the nation's electricity or telecommunications or oil. That monopoly might be operated by the state or by a private enterprise whose pricing and investment activities are regulated in a way to prevent excessive profits. The worst case is where a *private monopoly* exists that has given favors to government parties in return for installing barriers preventing any competitor from appearing.

There can also be an oligopoly of a few dominant firms that agree to price in a certain way and control output, following cartel-like principles. Cartels are found in such industries as oil, electricity, and telecommunications. They result in higher prices and reduced outputs. Another problem with oligopolies is the standardization of products and services, which ignores many buyers who want product and service variations.

Edmund S. Phelps, a professor of economics at Columbia University and a Nobel laureate, reports a troubling trend in many countries that he calls "corporatism," in which economic activity is controlled by large interest groups. When corporatism becomes dominant in a society, the public doesn't adequately appreciate the contributions of individuals who work hard to innovate. A corporatist economy can grow for a while, but it will not produce the needed growth that an entrepreneurial culture can deliver. The overconcentration of power in a small number of huge companies can lead to another type of market failure.

Even though dominant firms are in a good position to protect and perpetuate their dominance, other factors may finally end their dominance. A major one is the emergence of a new technology that is superior to the old technology. Kodak, which was unrivaled in the film business for a hundred years, lost its dominance with the rise of digital cameras that don't use film. Technological disruption often brings about lower prices that the dominant firm, so heavily invested in the old technology, can't match and where the cost of redesigning its whole business is prohibitively high. Besides technology breakthroughs, new competitors may win by launching a clever advertising campaign, or creating a substantially better product, or patenting something new. So in addition to possible government interventions to erase market failure, many other forces may come into play to correct a monopolistic situation.

there a contradiction between business objectives and environmental objectives?

There is a range of views on this question. Paul Hawken, an eminent ecologist, believes that businesses can adopt ecological practices without hurting their bottom line and, in fact, maybe improve their bottom line.[2] He emphasizes three things that companies must do: (1) end waste, (2) shift to renewable power (e.g., solar and hydro), and (3) create accountability and feedback.

At the other end of the spectrum, John Bellamy Foster, another well-known ecologist, views capitalism as intrinsically incapable of protecting the environment. He says if we want to save planet earth, we would have to change our system to socialism.

For much of American business history, businesses paid little or no attention to their impact on the environment. America had abundant land, trees, water, fish, and coal. The American mindset was to master nature and to exploit its seemingly infinite resources. As Americans moved west, wetlands were destroyed, deforestation was rampant, and prairie grasses were cut down to make room for growing crops. To increase the crop yield, pesticides such as DDT were sprayed to protect the crops against insects and diseases.

In the 1930s, the country experienced a terrible Dust Bowl, resulting from overplowing and the loss of rich topsoil, made worst by years of no rain. As our cities expanded, so did air and water pollution expand. Los Angeles's famous smog problem was produced by the rapid growth in the number of automobiles on the roads, allowing workers to commute over a huge territory. The fish in Lake Erie started to die because of dumped chemicals and other pollutants. Polar bears are struggling for life on melting icecaps as a result of climate change. And industry moves ahead installing more oil rigs in the Atlantic, ignoring the oil rig disasters in the Gulf Coast.

* * *

The existence of market failure is the reason for government intervention in a particular market. The aim is to find a possible means of correction. However, some regulations and types of interventions involving taxes, subsidies, bailouts, and wage and price controls may possibly lead to an inefficient allocation of resources, sometimes called government failure. This occurs when the cost of intervention exceeds the cost of correction. Usually political parties split on the issue of whether an intervention has improved on an inefficient market outcome or made it worse.

Market failures are a very common problem in a free market system. Conservative economists, such as the late Milton Friedman from the University of Chicago, argue that a market failure does not necessarily imply that government should attempt to solve the problem, because the costs of "government failure" might be worse than those of the market failure. Liberal economists feel that government should ensure efficiency and social justice through interventions or introduce market-oriented solutions.

SIX

ENVIRONMENT EXPLOITATION

I think the environment should be put in the category of our national security. Defense of our resources is just as important as defense abroad. Otherwise what is there to defend?

— ROBERT REDFORD

On November 2, 2014, the Intergovernmental Panel on Climate Change, consisting of scientists and other experts, warned that "failure to reduce emissions . . . could threaten society with food shortages, refugee crises, the flooding of major cities and entire island nations, the mass extinction of plants and animals, and a climate so drastically altered it might become dangerous for people to work or play outside during the hottest times of the year."[1] Is capitalism neutral in its effects on the natural environment and planet earth? Do companies produce and distribute their products and services in a way that is generally good for the environment or generally bad for the environment? If the latter, how can companies be motivated to adopt practices that will lead to a more sustainable world? Is

CLIMATE CHANGE AND ENERGY NEEDS

There remains a clash between climate change and energy needs. The United States has cheap coal deposits that can be burned and turned into electrical energy. But burning coal releases carbon dioxide (CO_2) into the atmosphere, causing a heat trap. This makes the weather warmer on earth and explains the melting icecaps. Melting icecaps cause the sea level to rise, threatening many coastal cities and leading to more dangerous hurricanes fed by warmer water and increasingly acidic oceans. Things will get worse if the earth's temperature rises more than two degrees centigrade.

The extra heat not only warms up the ocean but also pulls moisture from the soil, causing longer-lasting droughts. As trees and other vegetation dry, the frequency and size of fires also increase. Food crops such as corn, wheat, and rice are negatively impacted by heat stress. Such changes are pushing bacteria and disease-carrying species, like mosquitoes, ticks, and other pests, beyond their native ranges. There is so much animal and plant loss occurring that it threatens to eliminate 20 percent to 50 percent of all living species on earth in this century.

Clearly the solution is to reduce the pollution from coal and other fossil fuels and get energy from more neutral sources such as solar panels, wind turbines, and water power. The shift to renewables hurts the coal companies economically, and they will inevitably battle attempts in our courts to curtail use of coal. It also hurts consumers because these neutral energy sources cost more. This is one example of the many trade-offs involved in trying to meet the needs of commerce while protecting the environment.

THE RISE OF THE ENVIRONMENTAL MOVEMENT

Although most businesses paid little attention to the environment, there were always some lonely voices reminding us of nature's beauty and fragility. Henry David Thoreau taught us about the beauty of the woods and the flowers and the creatures. Walt Whitman wrote poetry celebrating nature. John Muir, the naturalist, urged us to protect the wilderness. His friendship with President Theodore Roosevelt helped produce our national parks movement. The Audubon Society, started and managed largely by women, was formed not only to protect birds, but to love nature. An ecology movement started in the 1920s, making us aware of the interdependence of nature, where every plant and animal species is connected with other species. In 1962, Rachel Carson wrote *Silent Spring*, about the danger to our water resources from pesticides and other chemicals flowing into them.[3] A movement toward environmental justice grew, urging us to live in more harmony with nature. The book *The Limits to Growth*, published in 1972, told us that the world's rapid growth in population and consumption could cause us to run out of essential, nonrenewable resources if we don't begin to practice care in the use of our resources.[4] Under President Richard Nixon, the Environmental Protection Agency (EPA) was set up to exercise some control over potential damage to the environment. Environmental groups, such as the Sierra Club, The Nature Conservancy, Friends of the Earth, Worldwatch Institute, and many others, staked out environmental areas in which they would exercise their vigilance and influence.

The result is that today, businesses and households are much more ecoconscious. Manufacturers now produce household appliances that list their energy consumption. Households sort their packaging into paper, glass, plastics, and garbage. There is increased interest and even profits to be made in reworking, reusing, and recycling. The EPA has required certain industries and companies to invest in pollution-control equipment to reduce the output of carbon emissions. That is the good news.

We are entering a new energy era with the process of fracking (where rock is fractured by hydraulically pressurized liquid to get at deep-rock gas and oil reserves) and the availability of cheap abundant natural gas.

Coal plants are shutting down. Four nuclear plants are being built. We are reducing our dependence on oil, which led in the past to our heavy military involvement in the Middle East.

Over thirteen countries—including China, Taiwan, South Korea, and Russia—are investing in building nuclear reactors as their preferred source of energy.[5] Nuclear energy will cause less damage to the world's climate and environment than oil but will pose the dangers of nuclear plant explosions and the disposition of nuclear waste material.

COMPANIES ADOPTING AN ECOLOGICAL CONSCIOUSNESS

Today, more than forty global banks, and many insurance companies, demand proper examination of ecological costs as a condition for funding or insurance coverage. More companies are finding it smart to move toward sustainable business practices. A company that acts sustainably considers the potential impact of its processes and products on the local environment and society as a whole. A good example is Timberland, a maker of outdoor clothing, equipment, and boots. Management at Timberland decides carefully on all the materials purchased and chooses only suppliers who themselves are practicing deep sustainability.

Another good example is the clothier Patagonia, which advises: "[We] aim to close the loop on the product life cycle—to make old clothes into new and keep them from ever reaching a landfill or incinerator. *Reduce* what you buy. *Repair* what you can. *Reuse* what you no longer need. *Recycle* what's worn out. *Reimagine* a world where we take only what nature can replace. . . . Together we can reduce our environmental footprint."

The late Ray C. Anderson, CEO of Interface Inc., the world's largest carpet-tile company, became an influential ecological advocate. At age 60, he read Paul Hawken's book, *The Ecology of Commerce*, and he suddenly saw himself as a plunderer. He decided never again to manufacture carpeting in the former wasteful way. He reinvented his worldwide factory operations and pleaded with other executives to reduce waste and carbon emissions. His company profits actually increased and he became a "recovered plunderer." "What started out as the right thing to do quickly became the smart thing. . . . Cost savings from eliminating waste alone have been $262 million," he told an audience of business executives. "We are all part of the continuum of humanity and life. We will have lived our brief span and either helped or hurt. . . . Which will it be?"[6]

Among the top 100 companies practicing sustainability are BASF, BMW, Bombardier, Siemens, and Samsung.[7] They have accepted that pursuing growth, profitability, and sustainability are compatible goals. But we need more companies, nonprofit organizations, and government units to join this movement. We are still far behind reaching the point where we can relax.

ENVIRONMENTAL PROBLEMS CONTINUE TO HAUNT US

In his book *Capitalism 3.0*, Peter Barnes says capitalism still produces environmental and social costs that are rising faster than the production benefits.[8] He claims that if we subtracted the environmental costs from our GDP, the net GDP might be half the size.

Tim Jackson, in his book *Prosperity Without Growth: Economics for a Finite Planet*, observes that while we are getting more production for any carbon we emit into the atmosphere (we have become 25 percent more efficient globally in the past forty years), our actual carbon output is up by 80 percent.[9] More people are finding more ways to burn fossil fuels. Jackson reports on our overuse of important materials such as copper, bauxite, and iron ore. He points out that if the rest of the world reached our economic level, world supplies would be exhausted within twenty years. He says we are addicted to wanting new products that themselves are constantly upgraded, leading to a "throwaway society."

Citizens have anxiety about being judged by what they own; they strive for acceptance by acquiring new things. Jackson sees the highly competitive capitalistic society as having one purpose: to sell "more." He concludes: "Prosperity for the few founded on ecological destruction and persistent social injustice is no foundation for a civilized society."[10]

The United States remains the world's second largest consumer of energy and materials after China. Our preference for beef over other food items makes for expensive land use, not to mention the added problems of high methane emissions and human obesity. Our preference for new products and their constant upgrading is also increasing the problem of how we dispose of our physical goods.

Activist Naomi Klein launched her diatribe against those denying climate change or who think we can live well with climate change in *This Changes Everything: Capitalism vs. The Climate* (Simon & Schuster, 2014). She says that free markets don't work when it comes to protecting public goods such as clean air and safe water. She sees greed in the fossil fuel companies and their supporting lobbyists and politicians who make lots of money exploiting the environment. She advocates much more local production as an alternative to buying goods from distant lands, such as China, which ends up consuming so much fuel and polluting the air. She calls for a new social movement of the magnitude of earlier movements that abolished slavery, colonialism, and other terrible conditions.

There is still much to be concerned about. *The Limits to Growth: The 30-Year Update* (published in 2004) reports that there has been a worsening of the environment since the influential book's original publication in 1972.[11] Here is a small sample of the environmental concerns cited:

- "Sea level has risen 10–20 cm since 1900. Most non-polar glaciers are retreating, and the extent and thickness of Arctic sea ice is decreasing in summer."

- "In 2002, the Food and Agriculture Organization of the UN estimated that 75 percent of the world's oceanic fisheries were fished at or beyond capacity. The North Atlantic cod fishery, fished sustainably for hundreds of years, has collapsed, and the cod species may have been pushed to biological extinction."
- "The first global assessment of soil loss, based on studies of hundreds of experts, found that 38 percent, or nearly 1.4 billion acres, of currently used agricultural land has been degraded."

WILL THE WORLD BE ABLE TO PRODUCE ENOUGH FOOD?

The earth's population is estimated to grow from 7 billion to 9 billion people by 2050.[12] The earth will have to support the production of enough food, animal feed, and biofuels to meet the population's growing needs. Here are the major problems in this area:

- The earth is losing arable land through top soil erosion, resulting from one-crop specialization and deforestation and city growth that removes arable land.
- Agriculture requires a great deal of water, which is diminishing as the planet heats up, water evaporation speeds up, and much water is wastefully used. According to the World Resources Institute, thirty-seven countries face "extremely high levels" of baseline water stress.[13] In these countries, companies, farms, and residents are highly vulnerable to even the slightest change in supply. Desalination of ocean water offers a big hope but is extremely costly in terms of energy and dollars.
- Agriculture is a major cause of water and air pollution through airborne germs and agricultural drain-offs. Agriculture causes 30 percent of our greenhouse gas emission.

- Much arable land is used to grow grass or soybeans for animal feed. Diets are getting richer in protein, which requires more resources than a vegetarian diet.
- Much grown food is wasted through spoilage during storage or shipment.
- People in developed countries consume much more food than is necessary, causing obesity and other problems.

Clearly citizens and governments must take more steps to improve food production. Some areas in the world have unused land that can be converted into arable land. Farmers must be taught more advanced methods of increasing the yields on arable land. More sources and uses of water and nutrients must be developed. Meat consumption should be reduced as a way to turn grasslands into more farm areas. The use of pesticides should be reduced and more use made of organic farming. Despite the warning from some environmental groups, accepting genetically modified foods would help protect more plants from the need for pesticides.

* * *

Here are the top ten environmental issues that business needs to consider:

1. Climate Change
2. Energy
3. Water
4. Biodiversity and Land Use
5. Chemicals, Toxics, and Heavy Metals
6. Air Pollution
7. Waste Management
8. Ozone Layer Depletion

9. Oceans and Fisheries

10. Deforestation

Each of these environmental issues has been discussed in dozens of books. Here are some of them: *Priority One: Together We Can Beat Global Warming*; *Water: The Fate of Our Most Precious Resource*; *Pandora's Poison: Chlorine, Health, and a New Environmental Strategy*; *Blue Frontier: Dispatches from America's Ocean Wilderness*; *The Blue Death: Disease, Disaster, and the Water We Drink*; *Natural Capitalism: Creating the Next Industrial Revolution*; *Sustainable Value Chain Management*; *Energy Management in Business*; and *The Business Leader's Guide to the Low-Carbon Economy*.

It has been documented that most investments to reduce environmental costs are recouped within twelve to eighteen months. As an example, 3M saved $1 billion in the first year alone on pollution reduction and, over the course of a decade, was able to reduce its pollution by 90 percent.[14]

The United States unfortunately lags behind many other countries in paying attention to climate change. Only 40 percent of Americans polled "strongly agreed" that the earth is getting warmer and thought that their politicians should fight global warming, compared to 75 percent of Brazilians. People in Germany, South Korea, India, Turkey, and several other countries also favor more steps to protect the earth.[15]

The real need is to convince businesses that sustainability is profitable, that sustainability creates a competitive advantage. Much of the pollution problem can be reduced if we manufacture lighter cars and especially electric-powered cars. We also need to rework our buildings and homes to be more energy efficient. We need to stop using coal and other carbon-intensive energy sources.

SEVEN

BUSINESS CYCLES AND ECONOMIC INSTABILITY

Watch the little things; a small leak will sink a great ship.

— BENJAMIN FRANKLIN

Businesses operate best when they have a clear picture of their target customers, their competitors, and the major demographic, economic, social, technological, and political forces affecting the broad business environment. Conversely, businesses operate poorly when many of those elements that deeply affect business performance are random and unpredictable.

There are two great injectors of risk and uncertainty into business decision making. One is the persisting presence of business cycles in capitalist economies. The other is the rising level of market turbulence in this new era of globalization and rapid technological development. Let's examine each in turn.

THE PROBLEM OF THE BUSINESS CYCLE

Business cycles seem to be an intrinsic feature in a capitalist market economy. From 1857 to today, the American economy has experienced thirty-three recessions. From 1960 until today, the United States experienced eight contractions (from peak to trough) of business activity.[1] The average contraction period from peak to trough lasted thirteen weeks. The average period from trough to peak took sixty-five weeks. As you can see, the contraction period is short, but the return to the next peak is five times as long.

The aim of economic policy is to keep the economy moving at a healthy growth rate. It should be able to create jobs for everyone who wants a job, and do so without causing inflation. This leads us to examine the following questions:

1. What are the phases of a business cycle?
2. What factors generally precipitate a business contraction?
3. What factors normally contribute to a more rapid recovery?

What Are the Phases of a Business Cycle?

A business cycle passes through four phases.[2]

Contraction. When the economy starts slowing down, it is usually accompanied by a bear market. GDP growth slows to the one to two percent level before actually turning negative.

Trough. While the economy continues to decline in a recession, GDP's negative performance each period eventually gets smaller and the economy gets ready to turn the corner.

Expansion. When the economy starts growing again, it's usually sig-
naled by a bull market. GDP growth turns positive again and should
be in the healthy 2 percent to 3 percent range. If the economy is managed well, it can stay in the expansion phase for years.

Peak. When the economy gets into a state of "irrational exuberance,"
with overly high expectations, inflation starts to appear. The peak
phase is when the economy's expansion slows. There is usually one
last healthy growth quarter before the recession starts. If the GDP
growth rate is 4 percent or higher for two or more quarters in a row,
the peak is just around the corner.

What Factors Generally Precipitate a Business Contraction?

Much of the business cycle is explained by changes in the level of business, investor, and consumer confidence. Periods of economic growth
occur when investors, businesses, and consumers have a positive outlook
on the economy. Consumers buy when they can depend on their income
level and home value. Even a little inflation can encourage consumers to
buy sooner before higher prices set it. High consumer demand leads
businesses to hire new workers and make further investments. Investors
may take on riskier investments to gain some extra return. There is
much capital and liquidity available, many people are making good
money, and everyone believes that the good times will continue. All this
suggests that the peak is not far off.

There are early signs that tell that an economy is getting overheated.
Usually there is too much borrowed money going into a major "hot"
area. The dot-com boom in the 1990s was followed by a dot-com bust
(1999–2001), when speculative investors realized that many of the new
dot-com companies were making little or no money. The next "hot" area
turned out to be the 2003–2006 boom in housing, with many mortgages

being taken by people without the means to pay them if they lost their job. In these two cases, consumer and investor debt increased substantially. The late MIT economist Charles Kindleberger said that bubbles can't exist without borrowing: "Economic disasters are almost always preceded by a large increase in household debt."[3]

Specific downturns can be precipitated by different combinations of factors. A contraction can start as a result of poor earnings, job cuts, major strikes, ballooning inventories, inflation fears, and other factors. Business, investor, and consumer confidence is shaken and the contraction phase begins. Investors start selling stocks, buying bonds and gold, and hoarding cash. The contraction is marked by businesses laying off workers and others hoarding cash rather than spending it. Stock prices fall drastically and inventories pile up.

Economists have long worked on the idea of putting together indicators of economic activities that would help predict changes in the economy. *Leading indicators* are those that change before a change occurs in economic activity. *Lagging indicators* are those that change after the economy has changed. *Coincident indicators* are those that change at approximately the same time as the whole economy. Among the indices used by these three indicators are earnings reports, the unemployment rate, the quits rate, housing starts, the consumer price index (a measure for inflation), industrial production, gross domestic product, bankruptcies, broadband Internet penetration, retail sales, stock market prices, and money supply changes.

What Factors Normally Contribute to a Recovery?

Each recovery has its own explanations, such as the role played by federal monetary and fiscal policy, business recovery success stories, good international news, and so on. Some people argue that new wars often end a depression: The Great Depression of the 1930s really ended with the beginning of World War II. In the midst of an ongoing recession, government does what it can to ease monetary policy, bringing down the interest rate to a level so low (called "quantitative easing") that businesses and consumers can easily borrow. But even when the interest rate is down to almost zero, it often isn't enough to stimulate a recovery. The debate then turns to fiscal policy and the use of taxes and incentives to stimulate the economy.

The big debate is about the best course of government policy. Here, two diametrically opposed positions battle. One—known as the *austerity solution*—states that the recession will eventually end on its own. Companies need to reduce their costs through cutting jobs and postponing investments. Workers need to accept lower wages if they want to hold on to their jobs. At some point, more companies will once again see opportunities to improve their profit and then the recession will be over. Europe tried this approach during the 2008–2011 period, and it made basket cases out of the PIGS countries (Portugal, Italy, Greece, and Spain)—partly because it was imposed on these countries, not chosen by them.

The other position is called *stimulus spending*. Here the government passes a stimulus spending bill such as legislated in the American Recovery and Reinvestment Act of 2009. The government essentially prints money to spend on needed construction, infrastructure improvement, and a variety of social needs. This puts money into the pockets of many people. Most of it gets spent and generates more money in other pockets. The stimulus spending in 2009 contributed to reducing the unemployment rate from 11 percent to 7.5 percent in three years.

Economists Atif Mian and Amir Sufi have suggested that contractions would be less severe if homes were financed with "shared-responsibility mortgages."[4] If home prices in a particular ZIP code fell by, say, 30 percent, the homeowner's monthly principal and interest would fall by 30 percent. If prices recover, payments go up but not above the original amount. The mortgage holder could be given, say, 5 percent of any capital gain that the homeowner realizes in selling the home.

THE PROBLEM OF HEIGHTENED MARKET TURBULENCE

Besides the risk and uncertainty that is introduced in different stages of the business cycle, another phenomenon has been occurring—that of heightened market turbulence.[5] In his book *The Age of Turbulence*,[6] Alan Greenspan describes his experiences as chairman of the Federal Reserve, where he had to deal with a great number of economic disturbances and shocks for which the only recourse was to muddle through and pray. He had to handle burgeoning trade deficits and retirement funding, as well as the proper role of government regulation.

The fact is that the world is more interconnected and interdependent than ever before. Globalization and technology have created a new level of *interlocking fragility* in the world economy. Globalization means that producers are increasingly importing resources from other countries and increasingly exporting their output to other countries. Technology—in the form of computers, the Internet, and mobile phones—enables information and communication to course through the world at lightning speed. News of a breakthrough discovery, a corporate scandal, or the death of a major figure is heard around the world almost instantly. While global interdependence works in everyone's favor in good times, it rapidly spreads much pain and damage in bad times. The good news is lower costs, but the bad news is increased vulnerability.

But what is turbulence? We know it when it occurs in nature. It creates havoc in the form of hurricanes, tornadoes, cyclones, or tsunamis. We experience turbulence in the air from time to time when a pilot asks us to fasten our seat belts. In all these cases, stability and predictability vanish only to be replaced by being buffeted, bounced, and jabbed by conflicting and relentless forces.

Business turbulence is defined as unpredictable and swift changes in an organization's external or internal environments, which affect its performance.[7] Yes, economies normally return to "normal" conditions, but in this new era turbulence at varying levels becomes a persistent factor.

A particular company or industry can be living through conditions of turbulence.

When he was the CEO of Intel, Andy Grove had to deal with all kinds of threats to damage Intel's preeminent position in the computer chip manufacturing business. It would take just one agile competitor to come out with a superior chip at a lower price to topple Intel. As Grove described in his book, *Only the Paranoid Survive*, he had to live with uncertainty. Intel had to erect an early-warning system that would reveal signs of imminent trouble. It had to create different what-if scenarios. And it had to preplan different responses to the different scenarios in case they occurred.[8]

Most companies operate with the assumption that there is a built-in self-restoring equilibrium. Economists built price theory with equilibrium in mind. If oversupply occurs, producers will cut their prices. Sales will increase, thus absorbing the oversupply. Conversely, if a shortage occurs, producers will raise their price to a level that will balance demand and supply. Equilibrium will prevail.

In our book *Chaotics* (AMACOM, 2009), my colleague, John Caslione, and I postulate that market turbulence is now the normal condition of industries, markets, and companies. Turbulence is the *new normality*, punctuated by periodic and intermittent spurts of prosperity and downturn. Today we can expect more big shocks and many painful disruptions, causing heightened levels of overall risk and uncertainty for businesses at both the macroeconomic level and the microeconomic level. On top of the everyday challenges of dealing in a perpetual competitive arena, as well as business cycles, business leaders need to recognize a heightened stream of major and minor disturbances challenging their business planning.

And turbulence has two major effects. One is vulnerability, against which companies need defensive armor. The other is opportunity, which needs to be exploited. Bad times are bad for many, but good for some.

But even when normalcy returns to the overall economy, it doesn't return to every industry or market or individual company. Hypercompetition operates continuously and relentlessly in normal times. The U.S. auto industry today is experiencing a *perfect storm* of high health care costs and enormous pension obligations converging with a weak demand for its products, which for decades have been seen as less attractive than foreign competitors' products. The airline industry is marked by too much capacity, and further consolidation is likely. Even without a global financial meltdown, times can be turbulent for specific industries and organizations.

Business owners and businesspeople have always lived with certain levels of turbulence in the business. This is normal and part of a normal economy. And in the past, broad economic swings lasting several years were an essential feature of the normal economy.

THE SOURCES OF TURBULENCE

We can identify and describe seven critical factors that raise the stakes for business risks:

- Technological Advances and the Information Revolution
- Disruptive Technologies and Innovations
- The "Rise of the Rest"
- Hypercompetition
- Sovereign Wealth Funds
- The Environment
- Customer Empowerment

Technological Advances and the Information Revolution

Information technology (IT) is one of the key driving factors in the process of globalization. Advances since the early 1990s in computer hardware, software, telecommunications, and digitization have led to the speedy transfer of data and knowledge throughout the entire world. The information revolution is probably the single greatest contributor driving and shaping the new global economy. Through the creation of interconnections with the potential to link all people and all business via a single medium—the Internet—the world's buyers and sellers can search, inquire, evaluate, and buy or sell from long distances. People do not need to limit their buying or selling to only their local area.

The Internet has transformed and globalized commerce, creating entirely new ways for buyers and sellers to conduct transactions, for businesses to manage the flow of production inputs and to market their products, and for job recruiters and job seekers to connect with each other. New media—websites, email, instant messaging, chat rooms, electronic bulletin boards, blogs, podcasts, webinars, cloud computing—create a global system that makes it much easier for people and businesses with common interests to find one another, to exchange information, and to collaborate.

But the information revolution contributes to the level of turbulence because there are so many more people sending and receiving messages about events in every country that can help or hurt different companies in different parts of the world. Enterprises need a key officer who can sample the stream of messages for trends, corrections, and problems that might affect the enterprise.

Disruptive Technologies and Innovations

Every company's business might be seriously disrupted suddenly or slowly by a new technology or innovation. The great Harvard economist Joseph Schumpeter pioneered research into how radical innovations lead to "creative destruction" and are necessary for a dynamic economy.[9]

More recently, Professor Clayton M. Christensen introduced the idea of "disruptive innovation" in a series of books.[10] A disruptive innovation can create dramatic change and render an older technology or way of doing business obsolete. Some disruptive technologies include mini steel mills replacing vertically integrated steel mills; digital photography replacing chemical photography; digital phones replacing traditional phones; and semiconductors replacing vacuum tubes. Disruptive technology has the potential to be the ultimate "game changer" that can create chaos in an entire industry, especially for the incumbents who haven't been paying attention to the turbulence swirling around them until it's too late.

Christensen postulates that "low-end disruption" occurs when the rate at which products improve exceeds the rate at which customers can adopt the new performance. Therefore, at some point the product's performance overshoots the needs of certain customer segments. Then, a disruptive technology may enter the market and provide a product that does not perform as well as the incumbent product, but exceeds the requirements of certain segments, thereby gaining a foothold in the market.

Once the disruptor has gained a foothold in this customer segment, it will proceed to exploit the technology in order to improve its profit margin. Typically, the incumbent does little to defend its share in a not-so-profitable segment and usually moves up-market to focus on more attractive, profitable customers. The incumbent is eventually squeezed into fewer markets until the disruptive technology finally meets the demands of the most profitable segment, ultimately driving the incumbent out of the market entirely.

In disruptive technology battles, disrupters usually win against older technology incumbents in the industry. One reason is an asymmetry in financial incentives. A disrupter may see a huge opportunity whereas the incumbent sees a much smaller one. Another reason why disrupters

usually win against incumbents is the fact that the larger, successful incumbent companies are organized into product divisions that often have
silos that don't communicate. R&D doesn't communicate enough with
design and development, production, marketing and sales, and business
development. This silo effect leads to a slow-moving ship instead of a
fast-moving speedboat. Collaboration across silos is slow. The disrupters
are looking at what customer needs are not being met, while the incumbents are focusing on the existing product.[11]

When attacked by a disrupter, the first reaction of executives in incumbent technology companies is usually to protect their high-paying
positions and their well-worn, comfortable business models. The typical
response: *Close your eyes and maybe it will go away*. But usually it does not
go away, and then the chaos really kicks in: Scramble to cut staff. Argue
and debate. And make it as difficult as possible for the customer to actually adopt the new technology.

Incumbents typically do everything in their power to put off the day
of technological reckoning. Their biggest problem is that they must bear
the burden of supporting the older technology and the business model
built around that technology, while at the same time experimenting with,
building up, and transitioning into the new business model structures.
Meanwhile, the technological disruptors do not bear this double-cost
burden. For disruptors, everything is fluid and relatively low cost.[12] And
while the incumbents are fighting to make sense of the chaos in which
they are so deeply mired, the disrupters are aggressively plowing for-
ward with the winds and waves of turbulence at their backs.

The "Rise of the Rest"

Another source of turbulence is the rise of other countries establishing
political and economic power in a global situation where until recently
the United States was the undisputed power. Fareed Zakaria's book *The*

Post-American World and the Rise of the Rest[13] attests to the world's rising emerging market powers, most notably the BRIC (Brazil, Russia, India, and China), along with Indonesia, Turkey, and the whole cash-rich Middle East. Europe became powerful in the 1500s, then the United States in the 1900s, and now Asia in the twenty-first century.

There are a rising number of competitors coming from emerging markets. Established Western multinationals will be confronting a growing number of emerging countries' multinationals.[14] A process of redistributing money and power—away from the U.S. and Europe and toward the resource-rich countries and rising industrialized nations in Asia and the rest of the emerging world—has been under way for years. They will be aggressively buying their way into the Fortune Global 500 with their acquisitions of leading Western companies—juicy acquisitions with their experienced global and local management teams and their established global brands.

Emerging-market companies such as Brazil's Petrobras and InBev, Russia's Gazprom and Severstal, India's Reliance and Tata, and China's Lenovo, Haier, Alibaba, and Huawei will increase turbulence and disruptions. These companies are growing at record paces. The pace at which they acquire Western firms will increase as the global recession takes a bigger toll on companies in North America and Europe than on those in emerging economies. In fact, in 2008, emerging-market contributions to the Fortune Global 500 stood at sixty-two, mostly from the BRIC countries, up from thirty-one in 2003, and they are set to rise rapidly. Based on current trends, emerging-market companies will account for one-third of the Fortune list within ten years.[15] These extremely ambitious and aggressive companies will do whatever it takes to beat competitors from developed economies and also in developing economies, since it's in the developed economies where the most robust profits are found.

Hypercompetition

Hypercompetition occurs when technologies or offerings are so new that standards and rules are in flux, resulting in competitive advantages that cannot be sustained. It is characterized by intense and rapid competitive moves, in which competitors must move quickly to build new advantages and erode the advantages of their rivals. Competitors thrive on speed and surprise to introduce more appealing or lower-cost products and cater to more fragmented customer tastes. The falling barriers to trade contribute to structural disequilibrium and to the dethronement of industry leaders.[16]

Richard D'Aveni, professor of business strategy at the Tuck School of Business at Dartmouth College and author of *Hypercompetition: Managing the Dynamics of Strategic Maneuvering*, argues that competitive advantage is no longer sustainable over the long haul.[17] Advantage is continually created, eroded, destroyed, and recreated through strategic maneuvering by those firms that disrupt markets and act as if there were no boundaries to entry. The way to go about winning today is to render the current market leader's competitive advantages obsolete.[18]

In the hypercompetitive environment, profits will be lower for firms failing to create new competitive positions faster than their old positions crumble, especially as the weight of their depreciated and costly strategies will prevent many of them from adapting and adopting new behaviors fast enough.

Sovereign Wealth Funds

The increase in sovereign wealth funds (SWFs) means more capital can move swiftly to areas of opportunity and out of areas of saturation, causing another source of turbulence. A sovereign wealth fund is an assemblage of stocks, bonds, property, precious metals, and other financial instruments. SWFs have been around for decades, but have increased dramatically since 2000. Some are held solely by central banks that accumulate the funds in the course of their management of a nation's banking system. This type of fund is usually of major economic and fiscal importance. Other SWFs are simply the state's savings, which are invested by various entities.[19] The largest SWFs are the Abu Dhabi Investment Authority, Norway Government Pension Fund, Saudi Arabia AMA Foreign Holdings, Singapore Investment Corporation, China SAFE Investment Company, Kuwait Investment Authority, China Investment Corporation (CIC), Russia National Welfare Fund, Hong Kong Monetary Authority, and Singapore Temasek Holdings.[20]

During the global financial crisis in 2008, several U.S. and European financial institutions avoided bankruptcy by accepting SWFs from the Chinese government and various Arab kingdoms.[21] This says a lot about the "rise of the rest" as well as which among those *rising* will be the key groups making waves in the new age.[22] Sovereign wealth funds gained worldwide exposure by investing in Wall Street financial firms, including Citigroup, Morgan Stanley, and Merrill Lynch, when those firms needed a cash infusion due to losses at the beginning of the subprime mortgage crisis in January 2008. The tremendous damage that surfaced from the crises in 2008 only accelerated the transformation process.

The wealthy state-owned investment funds of China, Singapore, Dubai, and Kuwait control assets of almost $4 trillion. They are in a formidable position to buy their way onto Wall Street and the major London and European exchanges in a big way, making big waves.

In mid-2008 U.S. lawmakers and congressional investigators went on record stating that the unregulated activity of SWFs and other speculators had contributed to the dramatic swing in oil prices, and that the massive investment pools run by foreign governments are among the biggest speculators in the trading of oil and other vital goods, such as corn and cotton, in the United States.[23] They can be seen as major sources of the heightened turbulence.

Latent fears about incredibly wealthy—and opaque—sovereign wealth funds will add to the inevitable rise in protectionist sentiment when there is a return to less financially turbulent times. This rise in fear will be further fueled by the inherent disdain that many Westerners have for oligarchic and state-led capitalism, both of which are prevalent in many emerging markets with the biggest SWFs.[24]

Ultimately, through corporate acquisitions and the investments of SWFs in the U.S., Europe, and other Western economies, the role of the state (often an undemocratic one) in the global economy is rapidly expanding, and with it the inevitable "push back" from Western governments and businesses, creating new sources of turbulence with which businesses will need to contend.

The Environment

Ecological groups pressuring businesses to pay more attention to the environment are also introducing turbulence. All companies are facing increased pressure to conserve scarce natural resources and reduce pollution to ward off global warming so that life on the planet is not irreparably damaged. The "green movement" is growing and gaining clout, and adds to the cost of doing business overall, irrespective of any investment returns. Citizens and companies are entreated to consume and invest more conscientiously in systems that conserve air, water, and energy. And though most companies would like to support the green movement, it isn't easy to prove that investments in environmental initiatives at the company level are actually bringing a return, especially for shareholders.

Most companies now recognize the growing markets for cleaner energy, water, food, and transportation. Many are already seeing bottom-line benefits from business strategies and innovation based on sustainable development. General Electric is one company, through its

Ecoimagination program, trying to profit by providing solutions to energy and pollution problems. More executives at companies such as Samsung, BASF, and BMW now see environmental issues as opportunities rather than risks.[25]

Because competitors are likely to invest in going green at different rates, this circumstance will, at least in the short term, favor those who skimp. In some markets, leveling the playing field may require more government regulation and enforcement. The overall effect will be to increase the level of turbulence within and across different industries. At first glance, the U.S. and Europe are likely to be competitively disadvantaged relative to less developed countries because the latter are less able and less likely to make and enforce "green" investments. The West may try to use this situation as an excuse to lessen its own investments, leading to an ecologically risky outcome for everyone.

Ultimately, the value of companies is likely to change as environmental factors begin to affect their performance. The short-term impact on cash flows may be limited, but it will eventually be significant in some industries. As nations and companies begin acting more aggressively to address environmental concerns, including potentially expensive systems to reduce carbon emissions, major shifts in the valuations of sectors and companies will start to become clearer and more predictable. A critical first step is to review and quantify a company's exposure to noncompliance with current or prospective regulatory measures (such as carbon pricing, new standards, taxes, and subsidies), new technology, and environmentally prompted changes in customer and consumer behavior. Business executives will have to ask how specific changes would affect a company's competitive position if other companies adopted new business models and moved more quickly to "green" business practices.[26]

Customer Empowerment

In the past, businesses dominated the information airwaves. They would send out volleys of powerful brand messages using radio, TV, newspapers, magazines, and billboards. If customers sought further information about a brand or a seller, they could only turn to their own experiences or to friends and family. Such "asymmetric" information was weighed in favor of the sellers.

In the last decade a revolution has occurred. Today's consumers continue to get advertising from sellers, but they also can survey hundreds of "friends" on Facebook or LinkedIn or Twitter. They can look up the reports on Angie's List or Zagat and learn what other businesses and people like themselves think of a company's products and services. Increasingly, each region or individual country around the world has its own new group of online, interactive sites connecting businesses and people to share experiences.

This means that customers and other stakeholders—employees, suppliers, and distributors—are no longer passive agents in the marketing process. They can learn as much about a company, product, or service as they choose. Beyond that, customers and all stakeholders can use what they have learned and tell others in their network by blogging, podcasting, emailing, or chatting.

The profound implication is that sellers who make substandard products or provide less than high-quality service will disappear faster than ever. The volume of word-of-mouth coming from businesses and people who have experienced a product or service will end up advertising the good guys and defeating the bad guys. And it will prod the good guys to get better and better. So customer and stakeholder empowerment acts as a catalyst leading to continuous improvement in the offerings of serious competitors.

By the same token, word-of-mouth has the potential to create turbulence and chaos for sellers. A person who experienced terrible service during a commercial flight can create a website devoted to the airline and welcome others with bad experiences to tell their tales. One irate customer or consumer can potentially undo an established company. Vigilant companies need to aim for high customer satisfaction and monitor the talk on the Internet to make sure that one angry individual doesn't destroy the company.

As customers increasingly demand greater input into how businesses interact with them, leading organizations of all sizes will gain advantages by transforming this increased customer involvement from risk to opportunity and long-term success.

*　*　*

The business cycle and heightened market turbulence are factors that greatly influence the performance of a market economy. I've described these factors as constituting a shortcoming of capitalism, but in fact they are an intrinsic part of any economic system. The Soviets claimed that their economic system had eliminated the business cycle, but all they were able to do was conceal it from their news media. Someone living in Moscow had little knowledge of the economic health or sickness of other regions of the Soviet Union.

The Soviets also could claim that their economy was not plagued with turbulence. After all, the economic system had eliminated class warfare by eliminating the rich. The proletariat was no longer exploited. They ruled the country. All Soviet ads and films applauded the New System and the harmony and hope that it generated.

The fact is that the business cycle and heightened turbulence characterize all economic systems, but these characteristics are particularly salient in a free and open market economy characterized by hypercompetition and rapid technological change. The real task is not to dream of eliminating the business cycle or turbulence, but to moderate their amplitude and impact so that economic decision makers can operate more rationally.

The business cycle can be moderated by improving the ability of those guiding the economy to recognize a bubble when it is forming and to take action to cool down the speculation and "irrational exuberance." And when a recession has occurred, those guiding the economy have to take quicker action to infuse money and credit into the market economy so that spending can start up again.

Heightened turbulence can also be moderated. More business enterprises are monitoring the latest data on consumers and their changing needs, expectations, and level of confidence. Businesses are more able to measure their standing (i.e., perceived value) in the minds of their target customers and respond to any dips in their standing. Businesses are watching their competitors more closely and evaluating their plans and their standing in the marketplace. No one expects that these steps will eliminate surprises coming from random and unpredictable events. But the keener knowledge of what is taking place will hopefully reduce the number of real surprises.

Having reviewed the main factors causing business cycle change and turbulence, businesses need *a new strategic framework* for operating in each phase of the business cycle and in each level of turbulence. When he wrote of turbulence during the deep recession in the early 1990s, Peter Drucker stated:

In turbulent times, an enterprise has to be managed *both* to withstand sudden blows and to avail itself of sudden unexpected opportunities. This means that in turbulent times the fundamentals have to be managed, and managed well.[27]

Businesses must develop the skills, systems, processes, and disciplines to quickly detect and predict changes in their environment, to identify their vulnerabilities and the opportunities that come from change, and to enable the business enterprise to respond wisely and with strong resolve. All business leaders are intensely focused on creating strategies, organizational structures, and company cultures that create and deliver superior customer value over the life of a business enterprise. In turbulent times, as Drucker noted, maximizing the creation of continuous value will require a new business outlook and set of behaviors.

While companies are gearing up for the greater turbulence and chaos that lie ahead, they will not soon forget the pain and the lessons of the 2008 financial meltdown. Companies will proceed more cautiously and adopt a risk-oriented mindset. Government will try to pass regulations to prevent a repeat of this kind of housing and mortgage bubble. Banks and companies will be less prone to sell their goods and services "with no money down." Credit practices will be monitored more carefully to avoid another "house of cards" economy.

The perennial drivers of globalization over the past fifty years, the United States and Europe, will no longer play their former dominant roles. A process of redistributing money and power around the world—away from the U.S. and Europe and toward the resource-rich countries and rising industrialized nations in Asia—has been under way since the 9/11 terrorist attacks, when China, Russia, the Middle East, and other rising economies began to accumulate tremendous hoards of cash as globalization soared, along with prices for oil, natural gas, and other commodities.

EIGHT

THE DANGERS OF NARROW SELF-INTEREST

It is not enough to be industrious; so are the ants. What are you industrious about?

— HENRY DAVID THOREAU

apitalism is an economic system that's largely rooted in the idea of individualism and individual rewards. People should be free to pursue their own dreams and build their own lives in a free marketplace. They shouldn't depend on the government or its handouts or even be beholden to public opinion on what is right or wrong.

Former Federal Reserve Bank Chairman Alan Greenspan put the question this way: "Do we wish a society of dependence on government or a society based on the self-reliance of individual citizens?" I would challenge his question and ask why we can't have a system of self-reliance as well as a system of community caring for families that need help. What is the best balance between the two?

THE CASE FOR INDIVIDUALISM AND SELF-RELIANCE

The extreme exponent of the individualism view was novelist and philosopher Ayn Rand. She wrote two famous books about her philosophy, which she calls *objectivism*. Her 1943 novel, *The Fountainhead*, portrays a young, strong-willed, and creative architect named Howard Roark who refuses to design buildings in the old historical styles.

He prefers obscurity to compromising his personal and artistic vision. He is a contrast to Peter Keating, another architect, who copies historical styles and joins a prestigious architectural firm where he uses flattery to rise quickly to a partnership in the firm. At one point, Peter Keating gives a commission to Roark to design a building for him. Roark agrees, provided the building is built exactly as he designed it. Roark later returns from a long business trip and finds that the building is finished, but it has been compromised. Roark dynamites the structure because it's not the building he designed. He faces a trial for his "crime."

Another character in the book, Ellsworth Toohey, is constantly critical of Roark's independence. Ayn Rand regards Toohey as the personification of evil, someone who embodies the spirit of collectivism, but actually uses it to gain power over others. Rand is against the ideals in Toohey's *ethical altruism* and uses the novel to make her case for *ethical egoism* (i.e., rational selfishness). Her hero, Howard Roark, is an uncompromising individualist who is bigger than life and worthy of hero-worship to Rand. Roark says: "I can find the joy only if I do my work in the best way possible to me. But the best is a matter of standards—and I set my own standards. I inherit nothing. I stand at the end of no tradition. I may, perhaps, stand at the beginning of one." Much of today's libertarian philosophy goes back to this idea of the free and creative individual whose enemies, namely socialists and collectivists, try to bridle and corrupt him.

Ayn Rand's second book, *Atlas Shrugged*, published in 1957, centers on a vision of a society in which its most productive citizens refuse to be exploited any longer by increasing taxation and government regulations. Business leaders, such as the steel leader Henry Rearden and the oil leader Elias Wyatt, shut down their respective industries and disappear. They join John Galt, the leader of this rebellion, to demonstrate that the destruction of the profit motive will lead to the collapse of society. Only if Galt, who represents reason, individualism, and capitalism, returns to society might the economy have a chance to be restored to its former energy and growth.

Rand attributes the destruction of society to the "looters and moochers." Looters take away the property belonging to the producers through force, such as by pointing a gun. Moochers, who create no value, take away the property of others by taxation, by demanding others' earnings on behalf of the needy.

Atlas Shrugged was an instant success when published and it stood on the *New York Times* bestseller list for twenty-two consecutive weeks. Although popular, it drew its share of critics, including Gore Vidal, who described the book's philosophy as "nearly perfect in its immorality," and Helen Beal Woodward, who felt that the novel was "shot through with hatred."

The late Ayn Rand to this day has a huge number of followers who see a pitched battle between those who value the individual and those who want individuals to submerge their interests to those of the greater community.

Rand's philosophy is somewhat captured in the 1987 movie *Wall Street*, when Gordon Gekko (played by Michael Douglas), the CEO of Teldar Paper, gives his famous "greed is good" speech: "Greed clarifies, cuts through, and captures the essence of the evolutionary spirit. Greed . . . has marked the upward surge of mankind."

Let's turn to less extreme examples of individualism to understand its origins and rationale. Individualism is the doctrine that values independence and self-reliance and believes that the interest of the individual takes precedence over the interests of the state or a social group. The concept of the individual arose in the Age of Enlightenment, which re-jected authoritarianism, obedience to kings, oppressive government, he-reditary status, established religion, and rigid dogma. The philosopher John Locke is credited with clarifying liberalism as a philosophy that "no one ought to harm another in his life, health, liberty, or possessions." Much later, the American Declaration of Independence was written. It includes the words (which echo Locke) that "all men are created equal; that they are endowed by their Creator with certain unalienable rights; that among these are life, liberty, and the pursuit of happiness; that to secure these rights, governments are instituted among men, deriving their just powers from the consent of the governed."

At the same time, in 1776, Adam Smith published his famous book *The Wealth of Nations*. He presented the case for the critical role of self-interest in driving an economy's growth. He was careful to call for *"enlightened* self-interest." Remember, Smith also wrote *The Theory of Moral Sentiments*, where he said morality and decency are prerequisites to capitalism. He would have dismissed the version of capitalism calling for "animal spirits" (a phrase made popular by British economist John Maynard Keynes) to lead the charge.

Among economists in the twentieth century making the modern case for individualism are Ludwig von Mises, Friedrich Hayek, and Milton Friedman. Von Mises was a leader in the Austrian School of Economics. He wrote *Liberalism* (1927) and said approvingly of Ayn Rand: "You have the courage to tell the masses what no politician told them: you are inferior and all the improvements in your conditions which you simply take for granted you owe to the efforts of men who are better than you."

Friedrich Hayek built partly on the work of von Mises and wrote *The Road to Serfdom* (1944), pointing out the danger of capitalism slip-ping into fascism in trying to avoid socialism. He was awarded the Nobel Memorial Prize in Economic Sciences in 1974. Milton Friedman wrote of Hayek, "There is no figure who had more of an influence . . . on the intellectuals behind the Iron Curtain than Friedrich Hayek. His books were translated and published by the underground and black market editions, read widely, and undoubtedly influenced the climate of opinion that ultimately brought about the collapse of the Soviet Union."

As for Milton Friedman, who received the Nobel Prize himself in 1976, he became the major exponent of individualism and free markets through his books *Capitalism and Freedom* (1962) and *Freedom to Choose* (1979).

THE CASE FOR COMMUNITY

Geert Hofstede is a well-known international scholar who classified different countries according to four cultural dimensions, one of which was "individualism vs. collectivism." He said in a collectivist society, such as Japan, the self-worth of an individual is rooted more in the social order than in individual achievement. A Japanese person would not want to stick out; if he does, he will be hammered down. "Shame" more than "guilt" operates in Japan and other collectivist societies; individuals must present a good "face" to others in their community. Community-oriented societies would include Confucian, Islamic, and Middle East societies to some extent. They all put a high value on social harmony, even to the extent of curtailing some individual rights.

Communism was one extreme. Countries that came under the communist philosophy held that action will be judged for its impact on the welfare of the masses, not on the freedom of individuals. The state was all important in making sure that greed and self-serving behavior didn't become the norm. Communism sought to own all the state's productive resources and all workers worked for the state.

Less extreme is the economic system known as socialism. Socialism emphasizes the "common good," allows private property and privately conducted economic activity, and strongly protects democratic institutions and elections. Sweden, France, and even Britain would call themselves socialist societies to different degrees.

I'd like to emphasize a difference between calling a society "collectivistic" and calling it "community-minded." The problem with an individualistic society is that many individuals will give little or no thought to the impact of their behavior on others in the society. They either ignore others in their decision making or don't care about others beyond their immediate family and friends. Individualistic thinking can lead to ignoring pollution, poverty, and other social ills, even though they ultimately affect the same individuals.

The other criticism is that individualistic values can result in many people in society experiencing anomie or alienation. In his book *Bowling Alone* (Simon & Schuster, 2000), Robert Putnam wrote about many people who bowl by themselves in a game that is supposed to be social. Although the number of people who bowl increased during the period he studied, the number bowling in leagues decreased. He laments the decline of "social capital" and points to other trends showing that Americans are less politically and civically involved, as indicated by low voter turnout, decreased participation in political parties, and an unwillingness to serve on committees. He believes that some of these trends are a result of more women moving into the workforce, which leaves them less time to do community service, and family members spending more time at home watching television or working on the Internet. Putnam laments the decline of social capital as posing a threat to the continuation of democracy.

The reaction to hyper-individualism has created growing interest in *communitarianism*. Its roots go back to the Hebrew Bible, the New Testament, and more recently socialist and union movement doctrines about worker solidarity. It can be found in Sidney and Beatrice Webb's concern for getting the British public to pay more attention to the poor and the working class. As a 2014 article pointed out, "The British government introduced free school meals for needy children in 1906, old-age pensions in 1908, funds to fight poverty in 1909, and national health insurance for the sick and unemployed in 1911."[1] The more individualistic United States did not move to welfare ideas until the 1930s.

The issue can be seen as making a choice between oppressive but nurturing communities (*Gemeinschaft*) and liberating but impersonal societies (*Gesellschaft*). Amitai Etzioni, a long-time professor of sociology at Columbia University, held that nurturing communities don't need to be oppressive. Etzioni founded the American communitarian movement in the early 1990s, which emphasized the importance of affect-laden relationships among groups and a shared set of values, norms, history, and meanings coming from a culture. Small towns have this type of community and involvement but larger cities, regions, and nations are likely to lose some of this "community" feeling.

Communitarians stress that individuals who are well integrated into communities are better able to reason and act in responsible ways than isolated individuals. Communitarians admit that there is a downside in that there may be high social pressure to conform and this can undermine the individual self. Individualists favor a neutral framework of rules where there may be a multiplicity of moral values, whereas communitarians might favor a more clear and shared set of rights, such as to universal health care, a free education, and a safe and clean environment. Communitarians were among the first to encourage people to support environmental causes, which they felt individualists ignored. Individualists would object by saying that environment protection violates their negative right to not have their private property taxed to support these causes.

Communitarians hold that neither individual rights nor the common good should take precedence over the other. The "good" society crafts a balance between liberty and social order, between individual rights and social responsibility. Communitarians reject the extremes of liberal individualism, on the one hand, and authoritarian collectivism, on the other. They say that a major function of the community is to preserve a "moral voice" as to what is right and good for individuals and the community. But they also stress that they do not want to return to traditional communities with their major faults: authoritarian power structure, stratification, and discrimination against minorities and women. Responsive communitarians seek to build communities based on open participation, dialogue, and truly shared values.

THE CONCEPT OF CORPORATE SOCIAL RESPONSIBILITY

Today, most companies are engaged in giving money to good causes. There are three rationales for this activity.

First, companies have received a lot of benefits from society, such as the roads, bridges, ports, and other infrastructure that helps them be profitable. Therefore, they should return something to society. Second, corporate social responsibility (CSR) helps improve the company's reputation as a good citizen. CSR will win over more customers and help employees feel better about their company. Third, giving to charity offsets the wide impression that companies care only about profits and about accumulating wealth.

There is a larger rationale called moral obligation. R. Edward Freeman made this point: "How are we going to make this company an instrument of service to society even as we fulfill our obligation to build shareholder wealth? . . . This country has been too steeped in materialism and self-centeredness. Companies need a soul."[2]

When a company decides to be generous, it must still decide who should get the donations. One possibility is to respond to the many good-cause solicitations that come from the community and other stakeholders, such as suppliers and dealers. The other possibility is for the company to choose an important cause and direct most of its donations to that cause. For example, Avon chose the cause of supporting research and treatment of breast cancer, an extremely important issue to women. In this way, Avon's reputation is strengthened for supporting a cause that most of its customers care about.

I am inclined to favor this focused approach to donation-giving. Nancy Lee and I studied this question by interviewing business leaders from twenty-five well-known multinational companies—among them IBM, Johnson & Johnson, Microsoft, American Express, Starbucks, Ben & Jerry's, Timberland, McDonald's, Motorola, Hewlett-Packard, and British Air—and asking them several questions, including: How did you decide on your cause? How do you measure the impact of your gift to know how much good it is doing for the receiving group? How do you measure how much your giving is doing for your reputation and attracting new customers and keeping present customers?

We published our results in our book *Corporate Social Responsibility: Doing the Most Good for Your Company and Your Cause.*[3] Here is a sample of companies and their causes: Kraft (reducing obesity), General Motors (traffic safety), Levi Strauss (preventing AIDS), Motorola (reducing solid waste), Shell (coastal cleanup), and Starbucks (protecting tropical rainforests).

Most of the companies paid active attention to measuring how the donations helped the recipients. The task of measuring the return to the company—in terms of stronger customer and employee results—remains more difficult because so many other variables also affect the company's reputation. In the end, one might say that helping others is a good enough reason and doesn't always have to be measured in dollar terms.

Our 2012 study called *Good Works!*[4] distinguished six ways in which a company can manifest its CSR: cause promotion, cause-related marketing, corporate social marketing, corporate philanthropy, community volunteering, and socially responsible business practices. For each of the six ways, we illustrate what exceptional companies, such as Starbucks, Whole Foods, Patagonia, Panera Bread, and others, are doing.

Another book of mine, *Market Your Way to Growth: Eight Ways to Win*,[5] describes how companies can use CSR as one of the eight winning growth strategies.

Simon Anholt, who developed a journal called *Place Branding and Public Diplomacy,* raised the question: Which countries contribute the most to the common good of the rest of the world? To answer this question, he researched and developed a Good Country Index made up of a country's standing on seven indices: science and technology, culture, international peace and security, world order, planet and climate, prosperity and equality, and health and well-being. Putting the data together from the United Nations and other international organizations, he scored countries to show whether they were a net creditor to mankind, put a burden on the planet, or fell somewhere in between. Here are the nine highest-scoring countries on his index (in order): Ireland, Finland, Switzerland, Netherlands, New Zealand, Sweden, Norway, Denmark, and Belgium. The United States stood at 21. At the other extreme of low "goodness" were Russia at 95 and China at 107. He drew the following conclusion: The more your country is good for the rest of the world, the more investment and confidence it will attract, the more it will collaborate with others, and the better it will compete and do well.[6]

*   *   *

It can't be said that capitalism intrinsically favors individualism over communitarianism, primarily because there are so many types of capitalism. American capitalism favors individual rights and the free market. European capitalism leans more to a communitarian position, as do Japanese and Chinese capitalism.

My own belief is that individual rights must be preserved and have a better chance of being preserved if they are accompanied by social responsibilities. In a world laden with major social problems—poverty, pollution, climate change, rising energy costs—individuals and companies need to show their concern by organizing to reduce these problems, lest they end up destroying the planet or bringing about violent revolutions. This is called by some "the Third Way" rather than favoring one philosophy over the other.

Yet the communitarian view is shared by only about 20 percent in the United States, according to a 2011 Gallup survey.[7] That poll reported that other Americans fell into the following groups: 17 percent expressed conservative views, 22 percent expressed libertarian views, 17 percent expressed centrist views, and 24 percent expressed liberal views. The U.S. public continues to carry a divided view over what is primary to a "good" and productive society.

NINE

THE DEBT BURDEN AND FINANCIAL REGULATION

*If you owe your bank a hundred pounds, you have a problem. But if
you owe a million, it has.*

—JOHN MAYNARD KEYNES

How do financial crises occur? In 2007, the American economy
was booming. People were making money. They were buying
homes and expensive cars. The stock market was active. Everyone planned to be wealthy.

But if you look more deeply, there were warning signs. Too much
borrowing, homes sold to people who couldn't afford them, greedy
banks eager to cash in, credit rating agencies overstating value, regulators not putting on the brakes, and then, suddenly, Lehman Brothers
collapsed, the financial system threatened to freeze, and the world economy began to lose trillions of dollars.

No one could determine any particular bank's risks. Because of derivative trading, a bank's value couldn't be assessed. Banks hesitated to
lend to other banks. No one could tell whether any particular financial
institution might suddenly implode.

BEFORE THE GREAT RECESSION IN 2008

The United States enjoyed a period of great economic growth and prosperity from 1945 to 1970. We thrived as the world's leading economic and military power. Part of our success came from the fact we were never invaded or bombed during World War II. WWII devastated much of the infrastructure of Europe and Asia. These countries turned to the U.S. for needed equipment, supplies, and food. Our manufacturing industry grew and prospered. Unions were strong. American workers got used to the idea of rising wages and rising consumption.

By the 1970s, many nations in Europe and Asia had managed to rebuild their infrastructure and manufacturing. Germany once again was building better cars and other goods, and commanding better prices. And Japan entered the U.S. market with cheaper and often better-made goods. Japan won market share increases in a number of industries, including automobiles, motorcycles, cameras, radios, watches, and small appliances. To compete, some U.S. companies moved overseas to make use of lower labor and material costs. This meant a loss of jobs in the U.S. In addition, women were increasingly entering the labor force. Immigration was also increasing, with many of the new arrivals accepting lower wages. All this led to an oversupply of labor that kept wages from rising. Unions, without the ability to extract higher wages from management, grew weaker and lost members.

Wages became stagnant starting in the mid-1970s. Workers responded to the flat wages by working longer hours and taking on more jobs. They ended up working 20 percent more hours, whereas the French were cutting down their workweek hours by the same level. American husbands and wives were both working and their older children were getting jobs at McDonald's. Americans still wanted to enjoy rising consumption, so they borrowed money to supplement their earnings. Initially they borrowed against their mortgages, which at least represented secured credit—namely, their homes. They later turned to credit cards, representing unsecured credit, to finance their consumer appetite, which continued to be fanned by heavy advertising. The result was growing consumer debt. For many workers, their debt was equal to their annual income.

The banks were loaded with money to lend to consumers. They actually pushed the money out even to those who couldn't easily pay it back with interest. General Motors, in seeking to sell more cars, created General Motors Acceptance Corporation (GMAC) to lend money to car buyers at a good profit. GM was happy to sell its cars for less and make it up in interest payments. GM became a bank as well as a car manufacturer and made more money on its interest payments than on its automobiles.

In the 1980s, the computer came into increasing use and killed numerous jobs held by secretaries and other office workers. Computers, along with advances in factory automation, delivered a big increase in company productivity and in company profits. Relatively flat wages plus growing productivity created high profits.

What happened to those growing profits? First, executive salaries steadily increased to the extent that now CEOs of many corporations are paid 200 or 300 times as much as the average worker, whose wages didn't increase. Second, some of the money goes into supporting politicians, political parties, and lobbyists to preserve or extend the benefits and privileges enjoyed by the rich capitalists. Third, some money goes into philanthropy to help those who suffer from poverty, low wages, or unemployment and to support hospitals, churches, museums, and performing arts organizations. Fourth, much of the rising profits goes into banks, where it can be lent to workers who need to borrow more money to keep up their consumption. Consumption becomes the payment to workers to compensate for poor treatment by their company. Ironically, instead of the workers sharing the good times with management and getting higher wages, they were instead getting the privilege of borrowing money that might have been theirs and paying it back with interest.

Today, the interest rate on credit-card borrowing is as high as 18 percent in many cases.[1]

THE U.S. GREAT RECESSION (2008–2011)

The U.S. experienced eleven economic downturns between 1945 and 2007, averaging about six years. They were called recessions and believed to be intrinsic to a capitalist economy of the American type. But the recession that started in 2008 was the most severe since the Great Depression of the 1930s.

The U.S. and the world economy experienced a disastrous financial crisis. A number of companies went under—Lehman Brothers and Bear Stearns being the most notable. Other companies were saved by the government throwing them a lifeline—AIG, Fannie Mae, Freddie Mac, and General Motors—as well as the government's $204 billion share purchase of several hundred banks. This doesn't include the $860 billion in stimulus money from the American Recovery and Reinvestment Act of 2009.

The government was criticized for saving companies and banks that were "too big to fail." There was an outcry in some quarters about "deficit financing" and predictions that it would lead to hyperinflation. Yet the fact is that the quick action by the Obama administration prevented the collapse of the economy. With further government spending through 2012 estimated at $4 trillion,[2] the unemployment rate dropped from 10 percent in 2009 to 7.3 percent in September 2013, and a gradual postrecession GDP growth of 2.2 percent was seen by the end of 2012. The stock market returned to the pre-financial-crisis level, largely due to profitable cost cutting and dividend increases from corporate cash reserves.

The U.S. economy is still stuck with tough problems to manage in the aftermath of the calamity. Taking into account the vast number of pre-financial-crisis employees who have dropped out of the labor market and the increase in part-time employment, instead of full-time employment, Gallup estimates underemployment (counting dropouts and part-time workers) of 17.2 percent for October 2013 as against an "official" unemployment rate of 7.5 percent.[3]

The current U.S. debt burden is extremely high and taxpayers aren't happy about the enormous interest payments on federal debt they must make to lenders to keep buying U.S. securities. U.S. interest payment on the federal debt is estimated, for 2013, at $416 billion,[4] or roughly 7 percent of federal revenues. "Uncle Sam will shell out more than $5 trillion in interest payments over the next decade," according to projections from the Congressional Budget Office. "Over the decade, more than 14 percent of all federal government revenue will be sucked up by interest payments."[5] I won't examine here the growth of state and local government debt.

There is no way this debt can be repaid. It would take the entire annual U.S. GDP to pay it off, which itself is impossible because there would be no economy left to generate the required GDP amount. The public fear of ever-greater debt warrants more public discussion. Many established economists say that there is no near-term reason to be alarmed. Paul Krugman leads in this view, saying if we work on job and income growth, we'll be in a better position to substantially reduce the debt. Other suggested solutions such as austerity are likely to impoverish the economy (consider the crisis in Greece) and make it even harder to ever pay down the debt. But most economists do recognize a mid-term and long-term crisis of spending growth in the face of a declining rate of GDP growth. Politically, we face widespread public and popular concern, since the magnitude of this problem exceeds any household comparisons used to comprehend this scale of repayment.

It's true that over 60 percent of this debt is owed domestically to the Fed, the banks, and pension funds. While these institutions will grow richer on the interest on their holdings, the American people realize that an ever-smaller percentage of U.S. revenue will be available for government operations, transfer payments (Social Security, Medicare, Medicaid), and social programs like education. Elected officials should not be allowed to get away with refusing to publicly address this problem. The Tea Party gained considerable power by insisting on large spending reductions, but the debate still rages over where cuts should be made.

There was a valiant attempt to officially address this issue in the 2010 Bowles-Simpson Deficit Commission, which recommended a $4 trillion deficit reduction for outlying years. This plan had no traction and remains today only a shadow of its original self. The sequestration of 2013 reduced spending authority on approximately $85.4 billion (vs. $42 billion in actual cash outlays) during fiscal year 2013. But in spite of these cuts, the Congressional Budget Office estimated that the total federal outlays will continue to increase, even with the sequester, by an average of $238.6 billion per year during the next decade.[6]

What about the danger of inflation? Although core inflation has remained under control, food, energy, health care premiums, and education costs are not included in the official U.S. inflation index. All of these and other nonindexed items far exceed core inflation. Many people believe that higher inflation is just around the corner and it will be impossible to pay down the high debt burden resulting from continued high spending/low tax policy of the past two presidential administrations.

GROWING INCOME INEQUALITY

There remains a giant concern about the growing income disparity (see Chapter 2). In 2012, the incomes of the top one percent rose nearly 20 percent compared with a one percent increase for the remaining 99 percent. The top 5 percent of households earned 22.3 percent of all the nation's income in 2012. The income of these highest-earning Americans has recovered completely from a fall after the financial crisis, compared with the 8 percent decline for the median American household.[7]

The middle class, which used to have some discretionary income and good credit, now finds the cost of college and the cost of health care to be significantly high for their incomes. This has made them more cautious in their spending. Many people worry about being able to remain in the middle class. The middle class has been the mainstay of the case for capitalism. Or is the middle class only an 1945–1970 aberration in the history of capitalism? Capitalists have to worry about a shrinking middle class and its possible threat to reducing or ending the privileges of the wealthy class.

Personal savings in the United States increased to 4.6 percent of income in August 2013. Higher savings combined with reduced spending keep businesses and jobs from expanding.

Consumer spending drives 70 percent of economic activity. Because of reduced spending, the Federal Reserve forecasts an estimated overall GDP growth of around 2.0 percent for 2013.[8] Despite three rounds of quantitative easing since 2008, there is not enough domestic spending to lift GDP to what the Feds consider a robust growth rate of 2.5 percent.

Two facts stand out. The first is that the United States, which stood as the largest creditor nation in 1970, is now the world's largest debtor nation. Second, the U.S. economy has undergone a radical transformation from being manufacturing-led in the past with a healthy number of employees earning a middle-class income to a financially driven economy where Wall Street and the financial sector holds the greatest share of assets and income. These financial sectors grow while the middle class dwindles. Banks, brokerage houses, investment banks, insurance companies, hedge funds, and others determine the future direction of the U.S. economy.

Manufacturing has dropped from 26 percent of all jobs in 1970 to just 9 percent in 2010. Trade, transport, and utilities jobs declined from roughly 21 percent to 16 percent of jobs. Calling these two sectors the "labor sector," we see a total decline from 47 percent of jobs to 25 percent. Even the percentage of government jobs declined by almost 2 percent, but we'll leave this finding out of our equation.

By contrast, financial services jobs increased from 15 percent to 22 percent in the same period; business and professional service jobs increased from 5 percent to 12.5 percent; and health services increased from roughly 4 percent to 8 percent of jobs during this same period. Let's call these last three sectors the "professional sector." From 1970 to 2010 the "professional sector increased from 24 percent of jobs to 42.5 percent of jobs (largely nonunionized).[9]

The difference between 47 percent of "labor" jobs, largely unionized, and 42.5 "professional" jobs, mostly not unionized, is a telling landscape of change in income and spending power, as well as income inequality. The range of income difference in the labor sector is far smaller than the range of income in the financial services and the business and professional sectors. "Professional" may sound like a higher paid job sector, but as a sector class it is on average lower paid than the "labor" sector of manufacturing and trade, utilities, and transport; and hence, in aggregate it has less consumer spending power.

The top 5 percent households that earned 22.3 percent of all the nation's income in 2012 are in the "professional" class, not the "labor" class. The top one percent income earners (minimum income of $350,000) are an investor class, not a consumer spending class.[10] The greatest portion of their income is invested in wealth management, not consumer goods and services. Members of this class may have several mansions and a yacht, but this is small potatoes compared to what they invest in financial products. Very little of this 22.3 percent of the nation's income flows into the real consumption economy.

While the numerous poor and middle class spend their income on 70 percent of the U.S. economy, the rich spend relatively little on consumption. This transformation manifests itself in three outstanding features of the economy: (1) the reduction in median income; (2) the historic declining annual rate of GDP growth; and (3) the declining percentage of the labor force to population.

These numbers are also a structural snapshot of the paradox of having income inequality and trying to increase national GDP. How can so many households with less real income than in the past spend enough to increase GDP more than in the past? The answer to the GDP riddle is consumer credit and personal debt for most households, notwithstanding the investment transactions of big money by the top one percent of households. Both of these sources of monetary circulation are the core activities of the growing financial service sector.

HOUSEHOLD DEBT

The national average wage index for 2011 was $42,979. Assuming that you have to have a job to get a credit card, we find that as of 2014, the average U.S. household credit-card debt, among credit-card-indebted households, stands at $15,607.[11] Compare this figure to 1970, when consumer credit was virtually zero. The blunt fact is that from 1970 to the present, the growth in consumer spending and GDP is a significant function of consumer credit debt, or other varieties of personal debt, rather than a rise in disposable income of labor. In short, most people who are denominated as middle class supplement their disposable income with credit cards. Over 50 percent of Americans have credit cards.

The sad fact is that U.S. citizens have a very low savings rate. Their savings rate was 4.6 percent in 2013. Contrast this with China where in 2012, the average Chinese family saved 50 percent of its income, despite rising incomes. In Western Europe, households also save. In 2012, Germany had an 11 percent savings rate; France had a 16.1 percent rate; and Norway, which has a higher per capita GDP ($54,947) than the U.S. ($54,101), has a savings rate of 8.1 percent. In spite of the fact that these other countries have cheap money, along with credit cards, mortgages, auto and personal loans, and low interest rates, they save more.

The temptation to buy is too great with credit cards and other financing schemes so readily available. Too many Americans buy lottery tickets with their almost zero chance of winning rather than put the same money into a savings account. I've heard the suggestion of offering a lottery chance tied to savings accounts, so the more money people keep in their savings account, the higher their chance of winning.

But easy consumer credit is not the greatest source of middle-class debt that drives 70 percent of the U.S. economy. As of 2010 average mortgage debt is $147,133 and average student loan debt is $31,509. From a U.S. household debt of nearly zero in the 1950s, American consumers reached a towering debt of $11.13 trillion by 2012, including $849.8 billion in credit-card debt; $7.81 trillion in mortgages; and $996.7 billion in student loans. Household debt as a percent of disposable income rose from 68 percent in 1980 to a peak of 128 percent in 2007, prior to dropping to 112 percent by 2011. Household debt as a percent of nominal GDP rose from 47 percent in 1980 to 77 percent in 2012. U.S. household debt rose from nearly zero in the 1950s to $12.9 trillion by the second quarter of 2012.[12]

Student loan indebtedness is moving higher, toward $1.2 trillion, and is now a burden for 40 million Americans who have at least one open student loan. This situation poses a considerable drag on the economy. Young people are not buying cars, homes, or furniture as they have in the past. Some can't get married because the other party doesn't want to assume a partner's student loan debt. This is seen as a major problem by economists. One proposed solution calls for student loan forgiveness, but this would put a major hole in the U.S. Treasury. Another proposal is to lower the interest rate on these loans. Some students still pay 7 percent on these loans, even though interest rates have dropped considerably in recent years. The argument is to cap all past and new student loans at 3.8 percent. This, too, will put a hole in the U.S. Treasury that would have to be filled by finding other tax sources. Another suggestion is that no person with a student loan has to pay back monthly more than 10 percent of their current income.

From a socioeconomic perspective, capitalism as practiced in the United States is really debtor-capitalism, rather than capital accumulation or saver-capitalism. Household debt of every type represents a rough average annual amount of consumption of at least 25 percent above disposable income. Rising debt explains how a declining median income can still generate a growing GDP!

Today, the median American household debt is $75,600. Twenty-five percent of Americans have no savings at all. A majority of Americans are not able to save anything from paycheck to paycheck. Approximately 35 percent of Americans are in debt collection after 180 days of failed payment. Today one out of six Americans receive food stamps, with 46 million Americans qualifying for food stamp debit cards and the average recipient receiving $150 worth of food stamps per month. Americans really don't have much more borrowing capacity to carry out further consumer spending.

A major function of capitalism is not only to generate jobs and household disposable income, but to market household debt to keep a 70 percent consumption economy going. Capitalism, which historically started as a credit system for enterprise supply, is now a debt system for household consumption. Capitalism's success depends on its ability to get people to "buy now, pay later." Capitalism has been able to market debt to households in spite of households having to pay high interest, sometimes 20 percent to 28 percent, on their credit-card debt. Note that this payment is made to banks and financial services, not to producers of goods.

We keep thinking that the key to economic growth is job and income creation, when in fact it is the ability to market debt to U.S. households. A monthly household debt index would be a better sign of economic growth than monthly unemployment figures. The economy can grow without employment growth. How else can we explain recent U.S. GDP growth of around 2.2 percent even though unemployment stays at around 7.4 percent?

There are signs today that banks are again pushing more debt on Americans who cannot afford it. An automobile company today advertises that its car can be purchased with a zero percent down payment and zero interest rate! A great number of Americans with shoddy credit are able to obtain subprime auto loans from used-car dealers even though they clearly won't be able to repay their loan and will end up having their car repossessed.[13] And the "payday industry" that makes short-term loans is getting people to borrow continuously at onerous fees. One payday company's manual instructs its employees to "create a sense of urgency" and offer the delinquent borrower the option of refinancing or extending the loan even after borrowers have said they can't afford to repay.[14] The newly established federal Consumer Financial Protection Bureau is busy formulating rules to protect borrowers from unscrupulous lenders so that we don't have another bubble burst on the scene.

THE FINANCIALIZATION OF THE AMERICAN ECONOMIC SYSTEM

Gary Hart, who once ran for U.S. president, shared an important insight on capitalism's unfortunate transformation:

> The confusion within the ranks of capitalism is stimulated by the shift in our economy from making and selling things to manipulation of money . . . and involves mergers and acquisitions, venture capitalism, leveraged buyouts, workouts and turnarounds, currency speculation, and arbitrage. While the money culture was booming . . . manufacturing was declining.[15]

Since the time of Gary Hart's statement, the U.S. financial industry has grown much larger relative to the U.S. GDP over the years. The

U.S. finance industry grew to 50 percent of the non-farm GDP by 2010. Income from the finance industry rose to 7.5 percent as a proportion of GDP and 20 percent of all corporate income.[16]

We have witnessed the growing role that Wall Street and financialization has played in creating booms and busts, most recently in the marketing of unsound mortgages, the excess lending with insufficient capital reserves, the issuance of the hard-to-understand derivatives, and the activities of hedge funds. Ralph Nader, a leading critic of corporate America, vented the strongest charge against banks for financing highly speculative investments, facilitating the takeover of companies and bilking their assets, helping companies move their assets abroad and leaving American workers without jobs, and paying themselves obscene salaries from profits in the process.[17]

One of the first moves to financialize the American economy occurred in 1996, when Citicorp planned to merge with the insurance company Travelers. Such a merger was illegal under the Glass-Steagall Act, which blocked banks from owning businesses in other financial sectors such as investment banking and insurance. Robert Rubin, then secretary of the treasury under President Bill Clinton, lobbied for removing the restrictions on banks, and a bill passed in 1999 with a heavy bipartisan majority voting to eliminate the Glass-Steagall Act. When Rubin left the Treasury Department exactly one day after the bill passed, he was hired by Citigroup for a salary of $15 million a year without any operating responsibilities.[18]

The financialization of the American economy is reinforced by the fact that the tax on long-term (over one year) capital gains is only 15 percent rather than the normal tax rate of 30 percent to 39 percent on earned income. Much of the earnings of the rich come from capital gains (also known as "unearned income") and account for people like Mitt Romney and Warren Buffett paying only 15 percent tax on their income when middle-class income earners pay 30 percent to 39 percent. The irony is that these financiers are not creating real goods and services, but earning money primarily from managing money.

Financialization is evidenced further by the large number of new types of products developed by innovative financial engineers. A major idea was "securitization," namely, the bundling-up of income streams such as credit-card and car-loan payments and mortgages, and then repackaging them as "asset-based" securities and selling them in "tranches" with varying levels of risk. Some of them included subprime mortgages of almost worthless quality. Add to this other derivatives and arcane and unregulated hedge funds that add another source of concern.

This is not to condemn all new financial products, especially those designed to create new insurance programs to cover currently uncovered risks. The term "missing markets" is used to describe some risks that should be covered, but so far there is no market to cover them. Robert Shiller, the Nobel Prize economist, described some of these "missing markets" in his book *The New Financial Order.*[19] He proposed that there should be a market in which a person could buy "livelihood insurance" to cover the possibility that his profession becomes obsolete or that his chosen profession was a mistake. Shiller proposed creating a "home equity insurance" market where people can buy insurance to guard against a decline in their home's value. He proposed "income-linked loans" where interest rates on loans would rise or fall with one's income, region, or profession. Not all of these ideas are practical, but they are designed to meet needs that currently present risks.[20]

The financialization of the American economy is further evidenced by the rapid growth of leading banks and investment houses, many of them called "too big to fail" at the time of the 2008 economic meltdown. In 1990, the five biggest U.S. banks held 9.67 percent of the financial assets of the banking system; by the end of 2013, the five biggest banks held 44 percent or $6.46 trillion, according to SNL Financial. In 1947, the financial sector represented only 2.5 percent of GDP. By 2006, it had risen to 8 percent. And during this decade, it averaged 41 percent of all the profits earned by U.S. businesses.[21] Historically, finance's share of the economy has become "a self-sustaining perpetual motion machine that extracts money from the rest of the economy."[22] A working paper titled "Too Much Finance?" published by the International Monetary Fund concluded that at high levels of financial debt, a larger financial sector is associated with less growth. A smaller financial sector might be desirable and reduce the chance of misallocation of capital and crisis.

Some suggest that the U.S. economy has moved from "pro-market" capitalism to "pro-business" cronyism. Thousands of lobbyists are engaged in influence peddling to get pro-business bills passed against the interests of the average citizen. Luigi Zingales, in his book *A Capitalism for the People: Recapturing the Lost Genius of American Prosperity*, asserts that the Occupy Wall Street and the Tea Party movements are actually aligned against the same opponent.[23] The Occupiers may focus their wrath on business and the Tea Party on government, but Zingales sees this as two sides of the same coin.

SOLUTIONS: MEASURES TO REGULATE THE FINANCIAL SYSTEM

If restructuring can't stop the large banks from being "too big to fail," the other answer is more regulation to limit their leverage and their movements into additional businesses. Neither Congress nor the White House has set up adequate restructuring and regulations to make sure the financial industry will not again go overboard in issuing junk securities and overextending credit, once more bringing down the whole economy. Unfortunately, there is currently a big lobbying movement to return to securitization without proper regulation.[24]

Let's consider what needs to be done to get the financial system to operate safely and profitably.[25] The first need is to make sure that no American banks become so big and important to the economy that we cannot allow them to fail. We can't rely on printing money to save these

banks at the cost of great taxpayer losses and unleashing a huge inflation.[26] These banks need to be broken up and forced to operate with
clearer limits on what different types of banks can do, distinguishing
between a savings bank, a retail/commercial bank, and an investment
bank, and preventing them from getting into other businesses, such as
insurance, travel, and the stock brokerage industry. Among the proposals are to restore the Glass-Steagall Act to separate commercial banking
from investment banking and from brokerage and insurance. The
banking industry opposes this move, especially given that investment
banking promises to yield a greater return, even given the greater risk,
than commercial banking. This may partly explain the reluctance of
commercial banks to lend money to small and medium-size businesses,
since the same money might yield greater returns when put into financing trading and investment activities.

Another proposal would be to require banks to back up more of their
lending operations with their own capital. Stanford University's Anat
Admati, in her book *The Bankers' New Clothes* with Martin Hellwig
(Princeton University Press, 2013), asks: Why are banks allowed to operate with 95 percent borrowed money when no other business can do
this? No wonder banks can grow too big to fail. She advocates that
banks should hold reserves of 20 percent to 30 percent to lend out as
their own money. This may result in banks lending out less and not
growing so big. She grants that banks might make fewer loans to small
businesses and that entrepreneurs would be less able to get bank funding. But slightly slower economic growth is better than the greater risk
of highly interconnected banks failing and dragging down the whole
economy. She is against bankers making enormous sums with little personal risk and taxpayers picking up the tab for their failures.

Paul Volcker, the former Federal Reserve Bank chairman, proposed
that government-insured commercial lending be separated from risky
trading operations by a bank. On December 10, 2013, federal regulatory
authorities adopted the Volcker Rule to ban banks from trading for their

own gain and limit their investment in hedge funds. The rule holds that markets, not individual bank depositors, should fund risky trading. The Federal Deposit Insurance Corporation (FDIC) insures bank deposits up to $250,000, and depositors should not be at risk. The basic idea is to require banks to have more capital available (and less leverage) to repay loans and withdrawals when needed.

Needless to say, the over 2,000 banking lobbyists have managed to stop some of these measures or blunt them by pushing for less money for regulation enforcement. Their aggressive and well-financed lobbying has prevented 60 percent of the Dodd-Frank Wall Street Reform rules from being enacted—rules that would make the banking system safer. The problem is that political candidates of both parties receive a lot of campaign funds from banking interests and are not likely to vote for curbing risky banking activities. In mid-December 2014, Congress rolled back a Dodd-Frank rule, making it possible for banks to engage again in derivatives.[27]

The second need is to do a better job of overseeing and regulating the new types of financial instruments that have come into the world's financial system. Derivatives, credit-default swaps, and various complex financial instruments—including money-market funds that are not FDIC insured—have been called potential weapons for mass financial destruction. Many investors and institutions don't fully understand these instruments, and any sudden drops in their value can create panic in the financial market. There is a need to determine which existing and new financial products are acceptable, so these products should be transparent regarding risk and return.

The third step is to drive banking back to its original purpose—meeting the needs and interests of small-, medium-, and large-scale businesses, both here and abroad. In spite of the huge amount of money in the hands of banks, many banks unduly limit their lending. Banks are cautious about lending to individuals or lending to businesses that need cash to cover costs or buy goods or invest in production. They're more comfortable using their money to buy U.S. Treasury bonds. They can pay the Federal Reserve a half percent a year to get the money they need printed by the Federal Reserve and then use this money to buy U.S. Treasury notes that yield 2 percent to 3 percent. There is no risk in earning this differential. Banks have also been lending money to stock traders, which partly explains the rise in share prices. In the meantime, these bank lending practices are not producing any output for improving the U.S. economy and the lives of ordinary people.

The largest banks don't want to bother dispensing small loans when they can make more money in high-frequency trading and global investment banking. There are too few smaller independent banks left to take an interest in financing local businesses. We may need to establish a separate type of bank to serve the small business market, just as the savings and loan banks of the past served the mortgage market.

The financial industry operates under many favorable conditions. For example, while there is a state sales tax on most purchases of products and services, there is no sales tax on financial transactions. If states could put even a one percent sales tax on the buying and selling of stocks and bonds, this could put needed billions of dollars into the coffers of cities and even tame down speculative fever.

Other suggestions include devising a better system for rating the creditworthiness of banks. The classic credit rating bureaus—Standard and Poor's, Moody's, and Fitch—completely missed seeing the financial risk that led to the Great Recession, partly because their income comes from the banks that they rate. We also need better qualified, higher paid regulators. We can't expect too much when we pay them in six figures while they are regulating banks and bank lawyers making seven and eight figures. We need to be harder on financiers who allow large bad loans to be made under their watch. Bankers should be put under the same Sarbanes-Oxley Act that requires CEOs to be responsible for big mistakes. Finally, when a bank sells questionable securities and buys insurance against these securities going sour, this should lead us to wonder why the bank should be selling these securities in the first place. Financiers should be liable for taking actions that might trigger financial crises.

* * *

Martin Wolf, the most astute financial economist with the *Financial Times*, stresses the urgent need for deep reforms in the financial system in his book *The Shifts and the Shocks: What We've Learned—and Have Still to Learn—from the Financial Crisis*. From endorsing in earlier days a strongly conservative view of financial freedom, Wolf has come around to worrying deeply about financial instability and rising inequality and the damage that they can do to democratic institutions. He has observed that another financial crisis could be so severe that "our open world economy could end in the fire."[28] Wolf favors higher capital requirements for financial institutions, less income inequality so that there is less credit growth, higher taxes on the rich, and higher Keynesian stimulus spending during recessions.

Echoing these concerns, Mark Carney, the governor of the Bank of England, told his audience at a May 27, 2014, conference on Inclusive Capitalism that banks operated "in a privileged heads-I-win-tails-you-lose bubble" and that "there was widespread rigging of benchmarks for personal gain."[29] Bankers receive big bonuses in good times, and usually receive their normal income in bad times. This can lead them into excessive risk-taking.

New York Fed President William Dudley proposed that instead of banks paying bonuses all in cash upfront, bonuses should be paid in installments over five years. If a bank got into difficulties, the deferred bonuses would be used to help recapitalize a restructured bank operation and also to pay any fines imposed on the bank.[30]

Clearly, when some of our most intelligent financial minds start calling for an urgent and deep reform of the present financial system, the time has come.

TEN

HOW POLITICS SUBVERTS ECONOMICS

The day the power of love overrules the love of power, the world will know peace.

—MAHATMA GANDHI

What is the relationship between the economic system called capitalism and the political system called democracy? Many believe that capitalism is the natural companion of democracy. But it depends on the type of capitalism. If capital is widely held by the citizens in the country, then citizens truly know their interests and can vote accordingly. But if capital is mostly in the hands of a few (say, in a country where one percent of the people own half of the capital), the democratic concept of "one person one vote" is a sham. U.S. capitalism today is essentially Corporate Capitalism. Capitalists are free to move their capital to wherever it will earn the most money for them. Corporate capitalists need not have loyalty to any community, state, or nation. Their interests can differ widely from the interests of the citizens. This one percent will have a disproportionate influence and impact on the country's policies and direction.[1] The issue, then, becomes whether democracy runs capitalism or capitalism runs democracy.

LOBBYING

"Lobbying" describes the effort of people representing a particular interest group to influence decisions made by government officials such as legislators, regulators, or judges. The term comes from the fact that "influence peddlers" would appear in the lobbies of legislative buildings to "buttonhole" legislators and influence their voting on behalf of the lobbyist's clients. Most lobbyists are lawyers and many are former congresspersons, senators, and government officials.

Lobbying takes place at every level of government, including federal, state, county, municipal, and local governments. In 1971, there were only 175 registered lobbying firms; in 2009, there were over 13,700 lobbyists spending more than $3.5 billion annually to influence legislators. Francis Fukuyama has labeled the U.S. system of government a "vetocracy" bordering on "interest group capitalism."[2] He sees lobbyists as representing a multitude of interest groups that dominate and direct the legislators on how to vote, making the executives (the president, governors, and mayors) fairly impotent. This causes the country to stultify and stagnate and miss the real issues affecting the future of the country.

Views About Lobbying

We tend to view lobbying activity as bad because it leads elected officials away from voting in the interests of the people in their district and toward voting in favor of the lobbyists' clients. We tend to see the influence of lobbyists as pernicious and favoring the interests of corporations and wealthy families over the common citizens.

Nevertheless, we must recognize instances of "good lobbying" by those trying to counter the misstatements and misinformation of other lobbyists and represent advocacy groups such as environmental, educational, and health care groups. For example, the American Medical Association lobbied Congress to pass laws against tobacco advertising or sales to minors, and most citizens would consider this to be a good lobbying effort.

In the "bad" category are the lobbyists for major industries, particularly oil, agriculture, pharmaceuticals, and defense. Lobbyists for the oil industry have managed to get the government to provide strong subsidies and privileges for that industry. Lobbyists for the agriculture industry basically serve the corporate owners of vast agricultural land rather than small farmers. Lobbyists for the pharmaceutical industry have helped achieve high drug prices in the United States by keeping out foreign drugs and delaying generic drugs. And lobbyists for the defense industry keep legislators actively voting for more military goods even when the military generals don't need or want them.

Campaign Financing

Campaign finance is the real source of corruption of our democratic ideal. Legislators face mounting costs to get elected or reelected—costs that are beyond their personal income and the income of friends and acquaintances. Each legislator needs campaign donations beyond what his or her political party can supply. Lobbyists are able to make campaign donations that come from their client corporations. Lobbyists cannot ask for the legislator's vote in return for a campaign donation. But clearly legislators will know the size of the donation and will want to somehow thank the lobbyists for the campaign support. Legislators also know that voting favorably for the interests of certain companies will increase their chances to become lobbyists after their legislative career is over. A congressperson can make several times his or her former annual salary of $187,000 by becoming a lobbyist.

All said, raising enough campaign finance money is a cancer that gets legislators to focus more on the interests of big corporations and wealthy families than on what best serves the interests of the voters in their district. Here is how economist Richard Wolff sees the relation between big politics and big wealth:

> A rather vicious cycle has been at work for years. Reduced taxes on the rich leave them with more money to influence politicians and politics. Their influence wins them further tax reductions, which gives them still more money to put to political use. When the loss of tax revenue from the rich worsens already strained government budgets, the rich press politicians to cut public services and government jobs and not even debate a return to the higher taxes the rich used to pay. So it goes. . . .[3]

We must recognize lobbying as essentially a marketing activity. The client hires a lobbyist with an issue in mind and the lobbyist identifies the key legislators, their voting tendencies, and their susceptibilities, all in order to develop the right information, communication, and persuasion strategy. Successful lobbying requires deft persuasion skill and therefore has much in common with such activities as management consulting, marketing, and public relations. Lobbyists hope to develop a close and trusting relation with various legislators and supply them with helpful information. Lobbyists must not commit the error of feeding dishonest facts to the legislator and thereby embarrassing the legislator, who will never again deal with that lobbyist. Although the facts they supply are usually correct, lobbyists put them into a context that favors voting a certain way.

Lobbyists often say that they don't approach a legislator and offer a political contribution. Most often the legislator phones them and asks for a political contribution, even stating the desired amount. The total cost of federal campaigns has skyrocketed in recent years, and elected officials today spend countless hours on the phone raising money for their campaigns. The real story here is not one of lobbyists corrupting some otherwise honest policymakers, but one of elected officials hitting on lobbyists in what resembles legalized extortion.

Lobbyists are paid a salary and given a budget to cover expenses and also contributions to legislator campaigns. One of the most damaging indictments of lobbying and campaign finance is found in Lawrence Lessig's book *Republic, Lost: How Money Corrupts Congress—and a Plan to Stop It*.[4] The U.S. Supreme Court decision in *Citizens United v. Federal Election Commission* ended up declaring that businesses were persons with a right to influence other citizens. The result is special interests funnel huge amounts of business money into influencing Congress and, therefore, business interests control the legislatures. Although there is little evidence of overt bribery, a lobbyist statement ("If you aren't able to vote for X, I'll have to contribute $1 million to your opponent") is likely to have a strong effect.

Does the lobbying activity really pay off? Some studies have tried to show that legislators were not overly influenced by campaign contributions. But Lessig shows that influence can occur in other ways, such as delaying or modifying certain bills or voting them down. He shows how legislators adjust their views in advance before asking for contributions, so there is no explicit evidence of a change in a legislator's view as a result of receiving contributions.

Other studies show lobbying has a great impact on congressional bills and policymaking. A 2011 meta-analysis of research findings found a positive correlation between corporate political activity and corporate performance.[5] A 2009 study found that lobbying brought a substantial return on investment, as much as 22,000% in some cases.[6]

Proposed Solutions to the Lobbying Problem

Clearly governments must pass laws regulating the influence of lobbyists. The activities of lobbyists must be reported and be free of overt bribery. Lobbying is subject to extensive rules that, if not followed, can lead to penalties, including jail. Yet lobbying is legal and is interpreted by court rulings as free speech, protected by the U.S. Constitution.

Among the solutions proposed are the following:

1. A cooling-off period that makes elected and nonelected government officials, members of their staff, and others wishing to enter the lobbying field wait a year or more before they can become lobbyists
2. Requiring lobbyists to register their contacts and expenditures and report which businesses and organizations lobby, how, to whom, and for how much
3. Establishing a ban on personal gifts
4. Putting a limit on campaign contribution amounts
5. Requiring political candidates to voluntarily agree to take only small ($100 maximum) contributions
6. Allowing federal tax payers to check off a certain amount to go to specific congressional candidates

BRIBERY AND CORRUPTION

Most fields have a dark side its practitioners hardly mention or deliberately bury. I've just described how lobbyists representing special interest groups attempt to influence legislators to vote on behalf of their clients. The tools that lobbyists use to influence legislators are all legal, except for one—namely, paying a direct bribe for their vote. Offering a payment to influence a vote or get a favor done is defined as bribery, and it is one of the main forms of corruption found around the world.

Bribery and corruption impose great costs to society. Corruption slows down economic development and burdens democratic institutions. People in power in countries rich in oil, gas, and minerals loot billions of dollars. Ships line up in ports and have to pay heavily for a chance to expedite the unloading of their cargoes. Honest businesses and citizens have to pay others who create no real value for the right to conduct business or handle their normal affairs. The result is a misallocation of resources because the most valuable and efficient transactions do not take place.

There are different levels of bribery, from small-time bribery to grand bribery. An Indian friend told me this story about small-time bribery. Clerks in the Sales Tax Office in India are supposed to give citizens forms to apply for sales tax registration. The Indian government gives the forms freely because it wants sales taxes to be paid. But a clerk told my friend that the forms were not available. Come back next week, he said. However, he would make the forms available for a small fee, which the clerk would keep for himself. My friend asked, "Why do you do this?" The clerk said salaries are low—and paying minor fees won't hurt those who have plenty of money. My friend asked another tax officer if this bribery practice bothered him. He said no. The salary is too small to let him send his children to a good private school. It has to be supplemented with a "little extra."

Even small-time continuous bribes can add up to a lot of money. My Indian friend told me about Sukh Ram, the Union Cabinet minister who had ties to the telecommunications industry and was caught with millions of rupees in his home. He adopted an air of injured innocence. "There are others who take far more than I have," he complained to the press. "Why don't they go after them first, rather than hound me?"

An example of a grand bribery is when Lockheed gave major bribes to buyer committee members in Japan who were choosing an aircraft. Or consider the African country where the president gave a personal loan to the country to save it from going bankrupt. But did anyone ask where the president got his money from? Did anyone ask where the late President Ferdinand Marcos of the Philippines and his family managed to accumulate such fabulous wealth? And what about Nigeria? This country is so oil rich that it now has the largest economy in Africa, but continues to have a vast number of poor people and a significant number of super-rich former army generals.

Bribery is a widespread practice, but I don't mention it in my textbooks. Why? I certainly don't advocate bribing the customer. Nor do I want to advise any company on how big a bribe they need to pay to win a particular contract. At best, I would want my students to know that one or more of their competitors may be offering bribes. They should report it to the authorities or desist from bidding.

I remember a professor friend at the London Business School who decided that the extensiveness of bribery as a practice needed to be exposed. He collected data during his executive management classes. He asked executives in his evening class to raise their hands if their company used bribery to win contracts. No hands were raised. Then he switched the question: "Raise your hands if you know that one or more of your competitors gives bribes." Almost all hands went up. The funny thing is the class contained managers from the same companies that didn't raise their hands when the first question was asked.

The professor went further and asked members of his class to send in anonymous descriptions of how specific bribery episodes were performed. He only wanted to know how the bribe was delivered in a specific situation. He received hundreds of cases over the years. He decided to codify the types of bribing arrangements and even figure out the best ways to bribe and optimal amounts to offer as a theoretical exercise. He planned to publish a book on his findings and told his wife. She panicked and warned him not to do it. He would get a reputation that would draw many unsavory characters to seek his advice on how to optimize on bribery. He decided not to write a book or article and locked away all of his research on the subject.

The terrible truth is that bribery is quite extensive. A business that is planning to enter another country should consult Transparency International to see how the country ranks in bribery and corruption. The Corruption Perceptions Index states the perceived levels of public sector corruption in 176 countries and territories around the world.[7] In 2012, the ten most corrupt countries were Somalia, North Korea, Afghanistan, Sudan, Myanmar, Uzbekistan, Turkmenistan, Iraq, Venezuela, and Haiti. These countries contrast sharply to the ten least corrupt countries: Denmark, Finland, New Zealand, Sweden, Singapore, Switzerland, Australia, Norway, Canada, and the Netherlands.

The fact that China and India are not mentioned in the top ten most corrupt countries does not mean that corruption is a minor problem in those countries. Actually it is a major problem, even though China ranks only No. 80 and India ranks No. 100 in the list of the 176 countries. Given the huge size of these two countries, corruption imposes a major burden on both of them. Even a relatively clean country, such as Germany, in the past allowed its businesspeople to write off any bribe they gave as an expense of doing business.

Most companies do not want to get into the bribery business to win contracts or facilitate performance. The problem is when a company knows that its competitor is engaging in bribery as a practice—should it offer a larger bribe, report what is going on, or desist from bidding?

Honest government ministers in poor countries are constantly offered bribes and saddled with bribery-accepting bureaucrats and venal military officers. The ruling elites sell their resources (e.g., oil, diamonds) to the highest bidders and put their ill-gotten gains into Swiss bank accounts, with little or none of this wealth going to the working class.

Proposed Solutions to Bribery and Corruption

Most corrupt nations have been ineffective in reducing corruption. One step they could take is to explicitly outlaw corruption and set high penalties on bribers. The U.S. passed the Foreign Corrupt Practices Act in 1977 so that any evidence of a corrupt act would lead to the perpetrators being heavily fined or jailed. On the whole, U.S. companies have behaved ethically under this law.

A second approach is to appoint a high-level government agency to investigate bribery occurrences and bring perpetrators to justice. This agency needs to run a public relations campaign against corruption and invite the public to report bribery incidents. The agency could even offer to pay whistleblowers who identify major bribing activity.

A third approach is to make it difficult for those who extract bribes to hide their ill-gotten money. Police and legislative effort is now moving to reach into the money-hiding centers of Switzerland and the Caribbean banks that manage ill-gotten money. The best piece of news is that many Swiss banks have agreed to pay taxes on the amount of money held in secret accounts. These banks are also facing increasing pressure to reveal the names behind large accounts.

GOVERNMENT REGULATION AND TAX POLICIES

A third way that politics can distort the outcomes of capitalism occurs when government interferes too much in the operation of the free market. Understandably, the government has to set up some regulatory agencies to ensure safe food, safe drugs, limited pollution, safe waste disposal, and safe public and private transportation. Economist John Kenneth Galbraith believed that economic regulation was necessary to keep the capitalist system fair and safe and to prevent large businesses from dominating the market. He saw government and unions as a needed "countervailing" force to prevent business excesses.[8]

The powers and responsibilities of regulatory government agencies are normally spelled out carefully. There should be provisions for bringing regulatory agencies to court if their power becomes excessive or abusive. Free-enterprise economists argue that much government regulation costs more than it's worth. Liberal economists take the position that businesses will cut corners to maximize their profits and business behavior must be monitored and regulated.

The other issue is that government must decide on sales and income tax policies. How much tax should be borne by the working class and how much by the wealthy class? The sales tax falls harder on low-income groups than if the same amount of tax dollars were raised through income tax. Poor people and lower income groups do not pay much in an income tax. There is the question of how steep taxes should be for the rich and super-rich. There is also the question of how much corporations and businesses should pay in taxes.

Conservatives argue that income taxes are too high and that leads to profligate government expenditures. They see too much spent on welfare and "entitlements." Liberals see entitlements spent on education and health and relief for the poor as necessary and desirable, and a way to make up for the excessive income disparity. Liberals point out the many tax loopholes and exemptions favoring companies and the rich at the expense of the poor.

Even the government's policies on foreign trade will have a deep impact on the welfare of different income groups. Low tariffs will benefit the poor in allowing lower-priced goods to enter the country. But it may mean lower employment at home because more goods will come in from abroad. How do we measure the net short-term and long-term impact on the poor coming from our foreign trade policies?

Clearly, government regulations and tax policies need to be subject to a periodic review process. Every regulation that is passed needs to include a stated time when the results of the regulation will be reviewed and the regulation might be revised or eliminated. Tax policies also require a frequent review to make sure that they are accomplishing the intended results and not depressing economic growth.

THE INFLUENCE OF THE SUPER-RICH

Finally, let's not discount the influence of the small group of very rich people in the country having a highly disproportionate influence on public policy. The Koch brothers spend billions of dollars to get Republicans elected. Sheldon Adelson, whose wealth is estimated at $22 billion, presides over a global empire of casinos, hotels, and convention centers. His fortune was the wellspring of financial support for Newt Gingrich in his run for the Republican nomination for president in 2012. Gingrich received over $17 million in political contributions from Adelson and his wife, Miriam, including $10 million in the last few weeks of the campaign for the nomination that went to a "super PAC" supporting Gingrich's candidacy.

Plutocrats give lie to the democratic ideal of one person, one vote. They want to desperately preserve and enhance their wealth and stop any efforts to increase their taxes. They refer to the "47 percent," which Mitt Romney alluded to when he was running for president, as lazy citizens preferring to live off food stamps and handouts rather than put in an honest day of work. They assume jobs are available to everyone who wants to work. They also feel they give a lot to charity and are not selfish about their wealth, although rarely do they demonstrate philanthropy on the scale of what Bill Gates and Warren Buffett are doing to improve the lives of others.

The main issue is that the super-rich have a major influence on who gets elected and what policies get passed in Congress. They can hire the best lobbyists and distribute campaign finance money to achieve their political agenda.

Proposed Solutions to the Influence of the Super-Rich

The most direct method of taming the wealth and influence of the one percent class is through more stringent tax systems. Here are possible measures:

1. Put higher taxes on luxury goods.
2. Pass a more progressive tax system, where the tax rate increases for higher incomes. For example, the tax may be 40 percent on an annual income between $100,000 and $500,000; 50 percent on an income between $500,000 and $1 million; and 60 percent on an income between $1 million and $5 million.
3. Set some agreed-on number so that, for example, no annual income can be more than $10 million. The excess will either go to the government or can be directed to some specific social problem.
4. When it comes to estate taxes, allow the surviving member of a family to retain $5 million without paying any taxes. The remainder can be distributed up to $2 million each to offspring (i.e., living children, grandchildren, and great grandchildren). Anything beyond this amount goes to the government.
5. Regarding gift taxes, allow the family to give an annual gift to family members of no more than $20,000 a year to each person. (Those receiving the gift must pay taxes on the gift.)

* * *

In his *Republic*, Plato described the original concept of democracy as a system of elected representation by an "enlightened electorate." Initially, women and slaves were excluded from voting. Over time, democracy morphed into the idea that every citizen can vote, whether rich or poor, man or woman, educated or not. Citizens only need to be able to sign their names. Many politicians have a strong interest in keeping voters ignorant and even buying their votes. Corruption is rampant in many "democracies." When we add the play of politics into the picture, the expected fruits of capitalism are further reduced. As shown in this chapter, politics distorts the outcomes of capitalism in four key ways:

- The role played by lobbying
- The extent and high cost of bribery and corruption
- The need for government regulations and appropriate taxing policies
- Dealing with the disproportionate power of the super-rich

Clearly all of these issues and proposed solutions warrant extensive research and discussion, although the partisan nature of our political system and the gridlock it has caused leaves little hope that this will happen any time soon.

ELEVEN

CAPITALISM'S SHORT-TERM ORIENTATION

The future depends on what you do today.

— MAHATMA GANDHI

Businesses operating in a capitalist market economy need to do dual planning. They must keep their eye on the short-term picture, making sure to achieve their growth and profit objectives. And they must implement their long-run investment plan for profitability, growth, and sustainability.

Both privately held enterprises and public utilities can do well with dual planning. Privately held enterprises are usually family-owned, and the plan is to pass on the business to children and grandchildren. The family avoids issuing public stock and therefore does not owe the public any quarterly or annual report on the company's revenue and profits. The family company is free to invest heavily for long-term success and may even lose money for some quarters in the short run.

The same can be said about public utilities. Gas, electric, and water utilities are under public scrutiny and regulation. They are set up to be currently profitable and investment-oriented toward the future. They must grow their facilities and output to meet future demand. Their profitability goal is agreed on by the regulators to be high enough to satisfy current investors and yet deep enough to ensure long-term growth.

Publicly traded companies, by contrast, have a distinct bias toward short-term planning and execution. Presumably, they have an understanding of investors' expectations for the coming period. If the corporation fails to meet their expectations, many investors are likely to sell their stock and move their money into more profitable businesses. Some investors may stay with a company during one or two disappointing years, but not much longer.

The management of a publicly traded company needs to share with its investors what it plans to achieve in the current period. A shortfall at the end of the period may lead the financial community to downgrade the company's stock and change its recommendation from a "buy" or "hold" to a "sell" position. The company will find its borrowing costs starting to rise. Management will do almost anything to avoid missing its targets. Senior executives are tempted to over-report sales in the present quarter, although there are laws against doing so. They may under-report current sales in good times in order to report these sales in the next quarter. Management wants to show a picture of smooth sales and profit growth rather than a picture of deficits and spikes from quarter to quarter.

The other problem is that stock markets are increasingly attracting investors and speculators who jump in and out of the market on short notice. So capital, instead of moving into long-term investment, is becoming more oriented toward short-term gains, leaving less capital available for long-term investment.

ON THE ISSUE OF LONG-TERM INVESTMENT

How much money can publicly traded companies plan to spend to meet their long-run investment needs? Clearly a company puts the first priority on achieving its short-term target revenue and profits. Hopefully, it will gain enough surplus income to invest in new product development and needed infrastructure. If cash is low for long-term investment, the company has the option of borrowing more money by issuing additional stocks and bonds. But long-term investment is clearly at the mercy of the company's short-term profit performance.

Capitalism's success in a country rides heavily on the quality of the country's physical infrastructure. Sadly, U.S. economic growth is terribly handicapped by the rusty state of our infrastructure.

The American Society of Civil Engineers (ASCE) issued an infrastructure report card in 2013. Patrick Natale, the ASCE executive director, lamented: "We really haven't had the leadership or will to take action on it. The bottom line is that a failing infrastructure cannot support a thriving economy."[1]

The ASCE gave grades to the condition of fifteen U.S. infrastructure entities. For example, roads got a D–, drinking water a D–, levees a D–, the national power grid a D+, rails a C–, bridges a C, and solid waste treatment got the highest grade, a C+. The ASCE estimates that the government and business would need to invest $2.2 trillion over five years simply to maintain the existing quality of our infrastructure. But under the current budget, the spending will be less than half that amount. Natale adds that "by underinvesting, the price tag escalates."

Several countries get much better grades, according to Norman F. Anderson, president and CEO of CG/LA Infrastructure. His survey showed that "[the United States's] ability to develop infrastructure projects [is] well below those of Brazil, India, China, and other countries with which we compete for scarce infrastructure dollars and expertise."[2]

The irony is that there is plenty of infrastructure construction occurring all around the world, but not in the United States. The only capital investment made in the U.S. on infrastructure that seems to pay its way is digital infrastructure, because there is service revenue from customers. But digital infrastructure is only a small fraction of the renewed infrastructure that the United States needs.

The late professor Hyman P. Minsky advanced the thesis that the tendency of American capitalism to focus on maximizing short-term profits has exacerbated the inherent instability of investment demand.[3] Speculators are drawn into financing long-term projects, but delays and other concerns eventually lead them to cash out, which introduces financial instability and eventually panic selling. Long-term corporate growth is sacrificed to short-term survivalist strategies. Growing financial fragility has had devastating consequences for both the West and the emerging economies.

MAINTAINING AND IMPROVING INFRASTRUCTURE

Let's remember the benefits that infrastructure contributes to an economy. High-level infrastructure lowers the costs of supply and gives greater competitive accessibility to more productive enterprises. Spending on infrastructure can increase employment, facilitate enterprise migration, integrate national regions, and support urban economic productivity and livability.

How is infrastructure to be maintained and improved in a short-term focused enterprise economy? Much of the infrastructure initiatives come from government at the local, state, and national level. Roads, schools, and bridges are usually the responsibility of cities and states. Unfortunately, cities and states are suffering from a budget crunch and many cannot push their capital borrowing any higher. The federal government, which needs to take care of fixing the electricity grid, preventing a cyberattack, improving our ports, reconstructing infrastructure lost in natural disasters, and so on, is handicapped by a dysfunctional political system that says no to any budget increases. Add the fact that in a democracy, elected officials can be voted out in as little as two years, which means they may be even less interested in supporting long-term projects.

Some corporations are in a good position to get the financing they need to enable large-scale investments. Many businesses form public-private partnerships (PPPs) to build or rebuild needed infrastructures. The PPPs will cover the cost of interest and capital repayment through public revenues, subsidies, and public debt.

Not only will improved infrastructure increase the nation's productivity, but the projects themselves would produce badly needed jobs. President Obama has pleaded for congressional cooperation to improve our infrastructure and create jobs, but current partisan politics has prevented it from happening.

In the past, the U.S. government managed to launch bold infrastructure projects. Consider the Panama Canal, the cross-continental railroad system, the cross-continental highways, the Tennessee Valley Authority (TVA), and other major projects. But today, one political side loudly tells everyone government is bad, government is our major problem, and government should shrink (except for the military). Meanwhile, our competitors, especially China, can develop dozens of new skyscrapers, ports, airports, and even new cities in the blink of an eye.

Consider the following example. The city of Suzhou in China decided to industrialize in the 1980s and build the necessary infrastructure. Today the Suzhou Industrial Park has grown to 288 square kilometers with several hundred multinational companies located at the park, including Siemens, Emerson, Bosch, Panasonic, GE, Bayer, Johnson & Johnson, Nokia, and Hydro, as well as many leading Chinese companies. There are over 15,000 foreign-invested companies in Suzhou Industrial Park. The planners developed a higher education zone within the park. Today, 40 Chinese and international universities are established within the education zone and supply tremendous talent to the companies within the park. This is what big-scale infrastructure planning can do.

Can an economy whose enterprises care primarily about quarterly profits and prefer to cap or reduce government spending nevertheless find a way to attract the capital it needs to repair the country's infrastructure and gain all the benefits flowing from high-level infrastructure? This is the $64 billion question.

The way CEOs are currently compensated has a lot to do with reinforcing companies' short-run profit obsession. CEOs receive stock options in their pay package to incentivize them to increase the value of their company's stock. As a result, they concentrate on building current revenue and holding down current costs. But the true measure of their contribution is whether their long-term projects will yield a rate of return higher than their cost of capital. In many cases, company stock prices have risen while capital projects have yielded a negative rate of return. This will eventually cause problems when the company can no longer pay dividends and its stock price falls. In addition, the company stock price often rises because of a rise in the whole market, which has nothing at all to do with the CEO's performance. Company boards need a better measure of the real value added by the CEO, not just whether the current stock price has appreciated.

*   *   *

Fortunately, some corporations have been able to avoid the excessive preoccupation with maximizing current shareholder wealth and do what is right to serve their stakeholders' long-term interests. As examples:

- Jeff Bezos of Amazon has held firm to his vision of making decisions that would benefit customers' interests, even against criticism that he could make more money in the short run.
- Jim Sinegal of Costco said no to financial advisers who said the company should raise its prices to make more money. He is not

interested in trading short-term profit for long-term growth and profitability.

- Howard Schultz of Starbucks is obsessive about delivering an outstanding customer experience and does not give in to short-term profit making.

- Richard Branson of the Virgin Group keeps his eye on increasing customer well-being through offering value, fun, and innovation.

- Acting Ikea President Rob Olson announced in 2014 that the furniture company will raise its average minimum wage from $9.17 an hour to $10.76 starting January 1, 2015. This 17 percent increase will go to the lower-paid half of Ikea's 11,000 employees at its thirty-eight U.S. stores. "It's driven from our vision of wanting to create a better everyday life for our coworkers," said Olson. This voluntary raise will also reduce employee turnover and bolster recruitment. Ikea has no plans to raise prices, cut staff, or reduce hiring.[4]

These companies are focused on building long-term enduring relationships with their customers, employees, shareholders, and the wider community, and are not fooled by short-term profit maximization. They provide evidence that high-pay companies can also be high-profit companies.

TWELVE

QUESTIONABLE MARKETING OUTPUTS

If you keep your eye on the profit, you're going to skimp on the product. But if you focus on making really great products, then the profits will follow.

—STEVE JOBS

One of the great things about American capitalism and freedom is that our economy produces an extraordinary variety of products and services. Our stores are well stocked with food, appliances, furniture, electronics, and everything else you can imagine or wish for. We have few laws stopping any products from being made, even if they may be injurious to health or safety.

ARE OUR FOODS HEALTHY?

Consider that in the last few years, the following books appeared:

Salt Sugar Fat: How the Food Giants Hooked Us by Michael Moss (Random House, 2013)

The Blood Sugar Solution: The Ultra Healthy Program for Losing Weight, Preventing Disease, and Feeling Great Now by Mark Hyman (Little, Brown, 2012)

Grain Brain: The Surprising Truth about Wheat, Carbs, and Sugar— Your Brain's Silent Killers by David Perlmutter with Kristin Loberg (Little, Brown, 2013)

These books assert two basic ideas: (1) A lot of the food we consume is unhealthy and (2) American and foreign manufacturers are ready to sell us anything that will make money for them. The irony is that the food industry is simply selling us the food we like. We happen to like salty, sweet, and fatty foods, and businesses are simply meeting our needs.

Isn't this also true of Coca-Cola and McDonald's, two of America's iconic companies? A bottle of regular Coke contains six ounces of sugar. Research shows a direct relationship between consumption of sugary drinks and an increase in obesity, which in turn promotes diabetes, heart disease, stroke, and many other health problems. A typical lunch at McDonald's includes a hamburger, French fries, and a Coke and is guaranteed to deliver a lot of salt and fat. The result is the rising level of obesity in the American and world population. But again, these two companies are not plotting to make us obese. They are only serving us what appeals to our taste buds. As long as we believe in producer freedom, we can't tell these giant companies what to make.

What's more, these companies are outstanding in their contributions to good causes. Coca-Cola not only sells us "happiness" but donates a lot of money to medical and community causes. As for McDonald's, there are 322 Ronald McDonald Houses in fifty-two countries where families with hospitalized children can stay free of hotel costs. Most Americans love these companies and their offerings.

There are times in American history when the government tried to ban certain products and services. The government undertook to ban alcoholic beverages during Prohibition only to finally end the effort, having created many criminal gangs and much public harm. The government is still conducting a War on Drugs, which is producing drug gangs and cartels without reducing the use of hard drugs. We didn't ban cigarette buying or smoking (although we've placed restrictions on where people can smoke), but we've put heavy taxes on cigarettes and limitations on their advertising.

WHAT ABOUT GUNS?

One of the most troublesome marketing outputs under capitalism is the widespread production and purchase of guns. Most nations have banned or curbed the public carrying of guns, with the glaring exception of the United States. The U.S. gun lobby (the National Rifle Association) is powerful, and most legislators are ready to accept the NRA's financial support in exchange for their voting to block curbs on gun purchases. Americans are able to buy not only semiautomatic handguns, but rapid-firing assault weapons. In some states, it's legal for gun owners to carry a gun into a mall, movie theater, or church. Gun owners claim a constitutional right to own and carry a gun on the grounds of the Second Amendment, which vaguely holds that citizens can bear arms. However, the constitutional intention was that members of a militia could carry arms, not individual citizens.

It is no surprise that as a result of the proliferation of guns, several tragic shootings have occurred, such as twenty-year-old Adam Lanza barging into Sandy Hook Elementary School in Newtown, Connecticut, on December 14, 2012, and killing twenty children and six adults and then killing himself.

One would think that the Sandy Hook outrage would lead to a flood of legislation to control guns. But since Sandy Hook, more pro-gun bills have been passed than those that were gun control bills. This is despite the fact that the American public is overwhelmingly in favor of gun control. Numerous organizations have been formed—the Educational Fund to Stop Gun Violence, Sandy Hook Promise, Moms Demand Action for Gun Sense in America, Mayors Against Illegal Guns, among others—to raise money and stop gun violence. They hope to be as effective as Mothers Against Drunk Driving (MADD) has been in bringing awareness to the tragedies caused by drunk drivers and helping to establish stricter policies on driving while under the influence. But legislators are afraid to vote for gun curbs, fearing the all-powerful NRA would use its money to defeat them in the next election.

THE ROLE OF ADVERTISING IN SHAPING OUR WANTS

Many influences shape our wants. Our family, nationality, social class, and genes are among the influencing factors. But the role of advertising should also be mentioned in turning our needs (say, for food) into wants (say, a steak).

One can say a lot of good things about the role of advertising. Advertising alerts us to a lot of products and services that we may need or enjoy. Advertising introduced us to the benefits of an electric refrigerator, when we used to spend time getting ice for our "icebox," and it introduced us to the electric dishwasher, when we used to hand wash and dry every dish. In that sense, advertising gets us to part with some money but we end up with a higher standard of living. Advertising also gives us better training for judging claims and counter claims about product attributes and virtues. And advertising makes it possible to enjoy, at no direct cost to us, expensively made radio and TV shows, thanks to sponsors wanting a few minutes of our attention.

Advertising, however, has its array of critics, including Thorstein Veblen, John Kenneth Galbraith, Daniel Bell, Vance Packard, and others who argue that the advertising industry is too powerful and uses every trick in the trade to get us to buy things that we don't need.

Here is a quote from an anonymous advertising man: "Having worked for years in the advertising industry, I can tell you that the manufacturing of envy, desire, and wantonness is in full swing. What are their fears? What are their hopes and dreams, their struggles? What makes them feel better?"

We are exposed to 5,000 or more advertising messages daily. We are shown shiny new cars, beautiful clothes, appetizing meals, and must-have electronics on a daily basis. We are told the subtle differences between products in the same category and often warned that something is on sale "for today only" if we act now. Thirty-second commercials are one-sided, never mentioning the downside of any product. Whole generations have been raised on the promises of the ad industry to make us more beautiful, more desirable, safer, and more satisfied.

The good news today is that the Internet and our cell phones have made it possible now to get two sides of the story. Our friends can share their preferences, experiences, and reservations about advertising claims. We can look up different reviews about products and brands on the Internet. We can even set up a personal blog and message our friends and others about vendors, products, and service quality. Books and information are readily available on sustainable living and sane consumption.[1]

Defenders of advertising will insist that they aren't manipulating us and that consumers have free choice. Here is the critic Benjamin Barber's answer to them:[2]

> One can easily argue that many people are making poor choices because they have been so deeply conditioned by advertisers. How can you justify spending 50K\$ on a car, and replacing it when it is 3 years old when an inexpensive well-made car will fulfill the basic needs of transportation and may last 5–8 years instead? How can you justify spending money on bottled water when tap water in most areas is

just fine? And how can you justify accumulating tens of thousands in consumer debt just to acquire all of this stuff?

Barber continues:

There is the paradigm that runs deeply through our society that having more money and having more material goods will somehow make you happier. The problem is that these desires can never be satisfied—there is always something more, and there is always someone else who has more. In the end all of this materialism leaves people feeling empty, and the only tonic that they know to try and fill the void is to go out and shop some more.

Barber goes further and breaks the process down into two stages. First, children are "consumerized" by ads directed at them and in their being included in frequent shopping trips. Second, adults are treated like children who need many products and who become defined by the brands that they choose. They see themselves as "I consume therefore I am."

There is another problem that intense advertising creates—namely, it gets people to want more things than their income can buy. And the finance industry stands ready to make easy loans and sells the idea, "Buy now, pay later." Everyone gets one or more credit cards and can quickly acquire a car, a new television set, and other "goods" by just signing on the dotted line. In 2008, a person with a $14,000 income was able to raise the money to buy a $708,000 home. College students now have a trillion-dollar debt incurred in getting their college education, where the tuition costs rise every year faster than inflation.

Banks don't have to worry about their easy lending policies. They can always repossess the home or car when there is a default. The banks can expect the government to help with student repayment of tuition loans. Somehow we have been seduced by advertising and banking to become an "instant gratification" society that itself contributes to over-purchasing, high debt, and a bubble economy that eventually bursts and continues the business cycle story of boom and bust.

THE QUESTION OF THE QUALITY OF PUBLIC GOODS AND SERVICES

Until now, I've commented on the quality of private goods and services produced in the American economy. The question can be asked whether public goods and services in America are generated at a high enough standard. Let's focus on two major areas: public education and public health.

First, consider public education. Public education in the United States is financed by local property taxes. The good news is that the local public can decide on what the educational needs are in its community, which may be very different from community to community. The bad news is that children living in communities that pay higher taxes will have access to better schools and schooling. Children living in poor communities, especially members of minority groups, are handicapped educationally. In the United States, only 38 percent of three-year-olds are enrolled in early education; in the Organization for Economic Cooperation and Development (OECD) nations, 70 percent are enrolled. The number of students in this country who are poor in math, science, history, and literature is appalling. A 2012 study measured the skills of Americans from the ages of 16 to 65 and found that they lacked the mathematical and technological knowledge, along with the literacy, of people in Japan and Northern European countries.[3] Our younger citizens were close to the bottom of the twenty-three nations the study assessed.

Next consider the U.S. health system. The United States spends a great deal more money than other countries on the health of its citizens and has much less to show for it. The United States spends two-and-a-half times more on health expenditure per person than the average of thirty-four other advanced countries in the OECD. For example, it spends twice as much as France, a country that is generally accepted as having very good health services.[4] Add the fact that before the Affordable Care Act was passed, over 45 percent of American citizens were without health insurance. When I shared this fact with a Swedish professor friend, he said: "Most Europeans are aghast at the American health system. The vast majority of Europeans consider basic health care insurance a human right and not as something for the free market. It is part of an infrastructure to make a country work, like roads."

* * *

What are the alternatives to getting healthier and safer products produced and consumed under capitalism? We have seen that bans don't generally work.

The first alternative is suggested by the cigarette example, where putting higher taxes on cigarettes reduced their sales. We could put higher taxes on items that are harmful to health or safety. Such taxes would most likely be passed on to consumers. But they would accomplish the goal of reducing consumption of these items.

The second alternative is to apply a "nudging" strategy, which involves loading the choices in a way likely to lead customers to buy the healthier alternatives.[5] Some studies show that high school students will end up eating healthier food if the healthier food items are put near the front of the cafeteria line. Students are usually hungry after classes and grab what they see first. Extending this idea further, we can imagine supermarkets such as Whole Foods giving better shelf positions to the healthier brands within each category. So, healthier cereals would be at eye level and cereals loaded with fat and sugar would be on the lower shelves.

A third alternative is to use "social marketing tools" to persuade people to make healthier choices.[6] The 4Ps (product, price, place, and promotion) could be applied to convince people about healthier and smarter choices. Advocates of better eating would describe the benefits of eating the right foods and the bad effects of eating unhealthy foods. Mayor Michael Bloomberg of New York City was the kind of civic leader who "counter-marketed" by trying to get supermarkets not to carry 16-ounce or larger sizes of sweetened drinks and ordering cigarettes to be put out of the sight of consumers.

A fourth alternative is to educate children from the time of their early schooling about making healthy food choices and stressing the problems caused by diets heavy in salt, sugar, and fats. Hopefully, their food choices would evolve more to the healthier offerings. This is the approach Sweden has typically tried to help its citizens grow up with the right habits and attitudes toward healthy living.

Many health charts exist showing the ingredients of a well-balanced diet that delivers enough vegetables and fruits as well as proteins and carbohydrates. The charts recommend getting more needed protein from fish and chicken than from meat. Beef, in particular, is an expensive way to get protein because cattle have to be raised on grazing land that is growing scarcer. Proteins, vitamins, and minerals can be delivered at much less cost.

THIRTEEN

SETTING THE RIGHT GDP GROWTH RATE

Life is like riding a bicycle—in order to keep your balance, you must keep moving.

— ALBERT EINSTEIN

Paul Polman, the brilliant CEO of Unilever, made the following statement: "Our ambitions are to double our business, but to do that while reducing our environmental impact and footprint.... It has to be done via more responsible consumption...."[1]

If all companies set the goal of doubling their business, and then they succeed, sustainability will be impossible to achieve. If the less developed countries would, by some miracle, achieve middle-class living standards, then pollution, road and air traffic, and energy power outages would smother our quality of life and our planet.

Medium and large businesses, especially those with stockholders, almost always set a growth goal, and for several reasons. First, the stockholders expect annual increases in revenue and earnings, which indicate the corporation is under good management that knows how to grow stockholder income. Second, a company's employees prefer a company that is expanding and thereby creating more opportunities for upward mobility. Third, business expansion permits spreading company fixed costs over a larger volume, bringing down unit costs that can be turned into lower prices or more profit per unit. Fourth, companies get rated by the media as well as the stock market for how well they're growing company revenue and profit. Fifth, the CEOs of many companies often are ambitious. They want to impress their peers with their business skills, which can lead to being invited to manage an even larger company and earn more money.

Most executives believe the company that doesn't grow will inevitably decline. The company will lose market share to more aggressive competitors. Competitors will enjoy further scale economies that will reduce their costs and increase their competitive advantage. A vicious circle will start where nongrowth-oriented firms get smaller and smaller.

Can a company grow forever? A few companies have managed to grow for one hundred years or more: DuPont, W. R. Grace, Mitsui, Sumitomo, Procter & Gamble, Siemens, Michelin, GE, GM, and Campbell Soup. But most companies go under much earlier.

There are three groups that see growth as becoming increasingly difficult and even advise businesses to downgrade company growth as a goal. One group, the Slow Growth Group, holds that many factors foretell of a permanent slowdown in the growth of most companies and countries, even if no public intervention efforts are made to slow down growth. Another group, the Sane Consumption Group, holds that government needs to introduce policies and regulations to limit the rate of growth if the planet is to remain functioning. A third group, the Steady-State Economy Group, holds that people would be better off if they stopped chasing consumption and lived with a steady economy.

Let's take a closer look at these three schools of thought.

SLOW GROWTH GROUP

I mentioned in Chapter 4 the forecast of Northwestern University economist Robert J. Gordon that U.S. GDP growth will probably be slow and not achieve the high levels of the past.[2] He would consider the United States to be lucky if its growth is even one percent in the coming years. He points to several "headwinds" that will slow down our growth: (1) the aging of the American population, (2) the stagnation in educational achievement, (3) the fiscal tightening to fix our public and private debt, (4) the costs of health care and energy, (5) the pressures of globalization, and (6) growing income inequality and the debt burden. He sees the generation of Americans now in their twenties as possibly doing worse than their parents.

But won't innovation save the national and world economy from slower growth? Past periods of stagnation were punctuated by major innovations such as the steam engine, trains, the automobile, the airplane, the telephone, radio, television, and the Internet. Can't this happen again? On this matter, there is no data to turn to. The great economist Joseph Schumpeter said you can never know when and where a major innovation will take place. If Gordon's slow growth view turns out to be right, then this nation and the world will have to look for other ways to generate well-being than through continuous economic expansion. Yet the lingering thought is that well-being comes from jobs, and most jobs come from company growth.

SANE CONSUMPTION GROUP

There is another group advocating that growth should be deliberately slowed down to avoid a natural calamity. Continuous growth is going to cause us to run out of certain nonrenewable resources and do terrible damage to our environment and the planet. In 1992, Donella H. Meadows, Dennis L. Meadows, and Jørgen Randers published a famous study called *The Limits to Growth*.[3] It was commissioned by the Club of Rome and compiled by an international team of experts. It used a computer model called World3, based on system dynamics, to analyze twelve scenarios of different possible patterns of growth and environmental outcomes of world development over two centuries, 1900 to 2100. The scenarios used different rates of population growth and different natural resource requirements to show the possibility of not only running out of certain nonrenewable resources and land and food shortages, but also severe environmental damage from air and water pollution and climate change.

The computer outputs of different scenarios showed many "overshoots" of the carrying capacity of the earth to support the level of consumption and the planet's sustainability. They showed that our one earth could not supply the resources needed by humanity and absorb the dangerous carbon footprint emissions.

The *Limits to Growth* study has been updated on two occasions with new features added in the way of feedback loops and new variables. Each time the findings grow more dire about the carrying capacity of the earth to sustain the consumption growth taking place without doing great harm to the planet and to people's expectations. We need to face the growing scarcity of water, dwindling oil supplies, deforestation, overfishing, global climate change, species extinction, pollution, urban congestion, and intensifying competition for remaining resources. It seems like the public prefers to keep its head in the sand than to favor taking actions to prevent a human and planetary crisis from occurring. The authors of *Limits to Growth* argue that many steps could be taken to reduce the overshoot and leave humanity with a good chance to lead happy and satisfying lives.

Chandran Nair, in his book *Consumptionomics: Asia's Role in Reshaping Capitalism and Saving the Planet*, takes an even more radical view on whether consumption-driven capitalism is a sound economic system for emerging nations. He warns that "in Asia, it can only deliver short-term wealth to a minority; in the long term, it can only deliver misery to all."[4] He estimates that the Western model of development would accelerate the harm done to our forests, water, soil, and fisheries. He would put curbs on consumption-oriented advertising and even thinks authoritarian governments on the Chinese model might be necessary to keep consumption from becoming excessive. He favors downsizing the financial industry, which has become too big and has strayed too much from its original purpose.

STEADY-STATE ECONOMY GROUP

What would be a blueprint for a nation, region, or city to live more simply and believe "Enough is enough"? The idea of a steady-state economy stands as an alternative to the idea of a growth-oriented economy. What is it? Why might it be a good idea? And how can a geographical location —city, state, region, or nation—shift its economy from growth orientation to a steady state?

Herman Daly and his "ecological economics" community have advocated that long-term sustainability requires the transition to a steady-state economy in which total GDP remains more or less constant. Daly defines a steady state as "an economy with constant stocks of people and artifacts, maintained at some desired, sufficient levels by low rates of maintenance 'throughput,' that is, by the lowest feasible flows of matter and energy from the first stage of production to the last stage of consumption. . . . A steady state economy, therefore, aims for stable or mildly fluctuating levels in population and consumption of energy and materials. Birth rates equal death rates, and production rates equal depreciation rates."[5]

A steady-state economy would solve the problem of not running out of needed resources and not polluting the earth. Its advocates are deeply concerned about the limits to the earth's carrying capacity. A steady-state economy seeks to deliver well-being to its citizens without pushing higher consumption. It not only emphasizes sane production and consumption, but also encourages more birth control and a fairer distribution of income. The poor would have enough to live on and the rich wouldn't waste resources by acquiring private planes, swimming pools, and large mansions.

The steady-state idea is somewhat utopian. How do you get a steady-state economy without most companies being in a steady state? Are we doing away with efficiency, technology change, competition, and private capital moving around the world? How do you deal with migration across borders, which is massive today? Do you close the borders? If there is no company growth, where would the jobs come from? The government will have to accept steady-state tax revenues while facing the increasing health care costs of aging. Public debt will have to grow.

It would be a tough challenge to achieve population stabilization. China has done so by enforcing a one-child policy, although currently it is easing its policy. Thailand has promoted the use of condoms and women's rights. The Ethiopian fertility rate dropped from 5.4 to 4.3 children after two years of people watching TV soap operas, which got them to think about how many children they wanted and the downside of having too many. Advanced economies like Japan, Italy, and Spain are already reproducing at less than a replacement rate; it's the same for the U.S. Most population growth in advanced economies comes from immigration—legal and illegal—rather than fertility of native citizens.

HOW TO CHANGE THE CULTURE OF CONSUMERISM

To get people less interested in an endless pursuit of consumption, other lifestyles need to be promoted: The value of relationships, the joy of nature, and the pleasure of a good community need to be stressed. But how do you achieve this type of culture change? After a century of instilling a consumer culture, it may take another century to undo it. I have no idea how, what, or who would drive this change. China's Mao Zedong made a culture change in a relatively short time by autocracy and a violent Cultural Revolution. Many steps would need to be considered and debated and may end up requiring a planned authoritarian economy. Here are some proposed measures:

- Establish limits on resource extraction.
- Set limits on total pollution.
- Put limits on advertising.
- Favor medium- and small-scale companies and nonprofit organizations.
- Increase local commons and support participative approaches in community decision making.
- Reduce working hours and facilitate volunteer work.
- Reuse empty housing and co-housing.
- Introduce a basic income guarantee and an income ceiling.
- Limit the exploitation of natural resources and preserve biodiversity and culture by regulations, taxes, and compensations.
- Transition from an automobile-based culture to one that encourages local biking and walking.

In spite of all these serious questions raised about a steady-state economy, there remains a strong "degrowth" movement that demands more than just sane consumption. It is anticapitalist and anticonsumerist. Degrowth thinkers and activists advocate downscaling of production and consumption, arguing that overconsumption lies at the root of long-term environmental issues and social inequalities. They believe that degrowth does not have to diminish the individual's well-being. "Degrowthists" aim to maximize happiness and well-being through nonconsumptive means—that is, by sharing work and consuming less while devoting more time to art, music, family, culture, and community.

It should be noted that degrowth is a prescription for advanced economies, not poor economies. Poor economies have no room for further reduction of consumption. For them, economic growth is appropriate and necessary.

Those advocating degrowth or managed decline encourage people to switch to living simpler lives in which people get their satisfaction less from consumption and more from relationships, nature, and community life. As one example, a movement in Catholic circles was started in the 1940s by a group known as the Detachers, who decided they would live more simply. The group included Senator Eugene McCarthy and his wife, the poet Robert Lowell, and Dorothy Day of the Catholic Worker movement. In Eugene McCarthy's words: "There was an ascetic movement in the Church . . . that held ideas such as 'Don't have an automobile,' 'Don't have a radio,' 'Sleep on the floor.'" Such extreme simplification is practiced by certain religious groups, such as the Amish, but the idea never took hold in the general population. There are measures far short of sleeping on the floor that people can adopt to help save the planet from catastrophe.

TWO MAJOR UNRESOLVED ISSUES

To get out of the growth-economy mindset, there are two major issues to address. The first has to do with jobs. The second has to do with corporate social responsibility for practicing sustainability.

The Question of Jobs

If we limit consumption, we reduce the number of jobs. It is bad enough that unskilled and skilled jobs are being destroyed by advancing technology. Making things worse, population continues to grow. There are too many countries where 20 percent to 30 percent of job-age youth can't find work. If consumer and business spending falls, it can only increase unemployment. Normally, we should be creating enough jobs to keep up with population growth and to compensate for productivity improvements.

In highly industrialized economies, competition stimulates technology improvements that increase labor productivity to reduce costs. As labor productivity increases, fewer people are required to produce the same goods. If growth stops, unemployment increases, household income drops, demand drops, and the system moves toward recession or depression.

Hence we face an impossible growth dilemma. Growth in its present form is unsustainable. But degrowth under present conditions will reduce consumer demand, increase unemployment, and lead to recession.

One possibility is to redirect investments away from consumer goods. We are already observing some decline among consumer goods producers and retailers, such as Sears, J.C. Penney, Best Buy, and others. More investment needs to move toward creating energy and water solutions and rebuilding the needed physical infrastructure of bridges, roads, ports, and sewage systems.

Corporate Support for Sustainability

Today's companies are expected to pay more attention to how their activities affect the environment. Some critics of GDP say that GDP is grossly overstated. We need to subtract the waste and pollution and other "bads" that companies have created, but not paid for. The net GDP might end up at half the officially stated size.

At the very least, a company should do no damage by way of air or water pollution. This alone might require companies to make large expenditures on pollution control devices. Beyond that, the company should choose suppliers and distributors who also conduct their business in an eco-friendly way. The company might even favor more federal regulations requiring that all companies be eco-friendly, so no competi tors can take advantage by avoiding these sustainability costs. But what can be done about foreign competitors that are neglecting sustainability? There is no global authority that can universally level the playing field.

We saw earlier that Paul Polman, CEO of Unilever, aimed to double Unilever's business, but to do it while reducing his company's environmental impact and footprint. Is he right in thinking that the business goals of "growth" and "green" are compatible? Probably, provided that the green gains come from the company reducing waste and doing more recycling, and thereby achieving real economic savings.

So far Polman has been successful in achieving Unilever growth goals and in practicing sustainability. Unilever is reducing greenhouse gases from manufacturing, transportation, and refrigeration; reducing waste and energy consumption in manufacturing; and reducing packaging waste through recycling.

Sustainability-driven companies such as Unilever introduce clear criteria to direct their new product development programs, invest more in reuse and recycling, and convince their stakeholders—employees, channels, suppliers, and investors—to reduce waste and accept some limits to growth. Such companies may have to change their compensation package to encourage their managers to set a better balance between the goals of growth and sustainability. The CEO needs to earn a payout based on achieving the planned growth rate while reducing environmental costs by a planned percent.

* * *

Realistically, each company has to set its own growth goal, taking into account the industry's growth rate, the country's growth rate, and other factors. Each company will hammer out a business plan to achieve its growth goal. But this raises a more basic question: Why must a company always plan to grow? Can't the company be satisfied staying the same size and still manage to earn good profits?

In fact, there are many small and medium-size businesses that don't adopt a growth goal. I dined once at an excellent small restaurant. I complimented the owner and asked whether he thought of opening a second and similar restaurant in another neighborhood. "No, I am satisfied operating one restaurant. Two would be a headache and three a disaster," he said. This restaurant owner favors a steady-state solution, not a growth solution.

Small businesses need to be cautious about committing to an aggressive growth goal. Such businesses generally have a deep knowledge of their current local market. To expand into new markets, these businesses will need to add more personnel and bear higher marketing research and advertising costs. They will end up facing bigger competitors who have bigger budgets. It might be wiser to use the money to find better ways to serve and expand in their local markets.

FOURTEEN

CREATING HAPPINESS AS WELL AS GOODS

The unexamined life is not worth living.

— SOCRATES

S uppose an economy manages to produce a high and steady rate of GDP growth. This sounds like an ideal economy. It would mean that per capita productivity is rising and there are potentially more goods and services for the citizens. But would citizens necessarily be happier? Would citizens attain a higher level of well-being?

French economist Daniel Cohen of Dauphine University raises the question: "Why is it getting harder to be happy, despite developed countries' increasing wealth? Why doesn't money make us happy?" He points out that French citizens are one-third less happy today than in 1950, although their income is twice as high. He answers his own question by saying that economics focuses us on *competition* while it is *cooperation* and free-giving that make us happy. He wonders if the time has come for developed economies to give up the idea of growth.

We have to distinguish the impact of economic growth on *happiness* and, separately, its impact on *well-being*. Happiness is the harder condition to measure. Happiness can fluctuate from day to day. Happiness is adversely affected by major events such as losing one's job, getting divorced, or having a major health problem. Happiness is positively improved when someone has good friends, is involved in a meaningful activity, and is making a difference in the lives of others.

We can ask people to indicate their happiness on a five-point scale where 1 equals very unhappy and 5 equals very happy. "Would you describe yourself as generally a very unhappy person (1) or a very happy person (5) or something in between (2, 3, or 4), most of the time?" Then we can try to measure how people's level of happiness correlates with various personal factors such as their background, religion, occupation, age, income, and so on.

Economist Richard Easterlin published a famous paper in 1974 entitled "Does Economic Growth Improve the Human Lot?"[1] After comparing per capita incomes and self-reported levels of happiness across several countries, he didn't find a correlation. He even found certain countries with some of the poorest people were the happiest. In later research, he found that within a given society, the very poor are generally unhappy and the very rich are quite happy, but he found little correlation at intermediate levels. Happiness at a national level does not continue to increase with added wealth once people have enough money to satisfy their basic needs.

First, happiness is partly conditioned by a person's genes, with some people born with a positive outlook on life and others with a negative or depressed view of life.

Second, happiness is partly conditioned by the religious and cultural character of the country. Having a positive outlook on life may have something to do with whether the person is Catholic, Protestant, Jewish, Hindu, Muslim, or some other religion. A person's outlook may also depend on whether finding a job and earning a living in a particular society is generally hard or easy.

As a U.S. family's income approaches $75,000, the family's happiness increases. They are less worried about having enough income to acquire sufficient food, clothing, and shelter. As incomes rise above $75,000, however, the likely level of happiness is no longer correlated with income. A millionaire may be unhappy because he wants to reach a much higher level of income. A billionaire may be unhappy because he needs to spend a lot of time managing his money and making sure he's not being cheated by his assistants.

Assessing a person's *well-being* rather than the person's *happiness* puts the question on a more solid ground. Well-being is a function of having a sufficient level of food, clothing, and shelter; being healthy; being educated; and having a job and skills. Once the variables are specified, it is simpler to more objectively measure a person's well-being.

We would expect that persons who have a high level of well-being would also show a high level of happiness. But there can be qualifications:

- Persons with a high level of well-being may be unhappy because they become jealous when comparing themselves with other people. Thorsten Veblen, the famous economist, talked about the pain of envying the social standing or conspicuous consumption of others.[2]
- Persons with a high level of well-being may be unhappy because they have not found a higher purpose in life or they haven't developed certain skills they craved or certain relationships they sought.

The reason for making this distinction between well-being and happiness is that citizens have to decide what they think is the primary goal of economic development. Is it to create more and more goods and services? Is it to create a happy citizenry? Or is it to create a high level of well-being in the society?

Most economists prefer to avoid these choices and simply rely on measuring an economy's performance by its rate of GDP growth. But here are the main problems of interpreting GDP growth as implying an improvement in people's happiness or well-being:

1. GDP growth says nothing about how the benefits of higher growth are distributed. We can imagine high GDP growth with the poor becoming poorer and the rich becoming richer. Only if GDP growth consisted of income growth for everyone could we say that the benefit is well distributed.

2. GDP growth means that the marketed output of goods and services grew, but it doesn't say anything about the quality of the output. Economist John Kenneth Galbraith noted that "an increased supply of educational services has a standing in the total not different in kind from an increased output of television receivers."[3] Growth in cigarette and alcohol consumption does not mean a growth in well-being, although it may sometimes mean a growth in temporary happiness. Growth in the amount of litigation taking place in society does not necessarily mean a net increase in the sum of happiness because one party's gain is the other party's loss. Growth in the amount of financial transactions may mean a lot of wealth is transferring over to property owners. Growth in the number of brands within a category doesn't mean higher satisfaction if all the brands are essentially the same. Growth in the production and stockpiling of munitions normally does not improve anyone's life and is similar to building pyramids. The point is that many GDP activities do not contribute to more happiness or well-being.

3. GDP growth ignores the costs that have been incurred with that growth. Consider that more GDP probably increases the level of air and water pollution and more traffic congestion. Consider

that GDP growth could be the result of more people working longer hours and having less leisure time.

We must remember that an average says nothing about the distribution around the average. We would want to judge the economy's performance by the level and trend of income inequality. If the wealthiest one percent of the U.S. population receives 28 percent of the U.S. national income, we can question whether this distribution is equitable.

We can judge an economy's performance by examining the poverty level in a country. Today 15 percent of U.S. citizens fall below the U.S.-defined poverty level. A family of three (two parents and one child) in the United States would have to earn more than $19,530 to avoid falling into the poverty class. In Sweden, a much smaller percent of the Swedish population falls below the country's defined poverty level. We would expect Swedish citizens to feel better off than U.S. citizens on the average.

GROSS NATIONAL HAPPINESS

In 1972, King Jigme Singye Wangchuck of the little nation of Bhutan proposed the need for a new measure called the Gross National Happiness (GNH) to be viewed alongside with the GDP measure.[4] The GNH received a lot of publicity and today countries such as England, France, Denmark, Brazil, and others are engaged in developing a GNH measure.

King Wangchuck took the point of view that happiness occurs when material and spiritual development occur together and reinforce each other. He postulated four pillars of GNH: sustainable development, preservation and promotion of cultural values, conservation of the natural environment, and establishment of good governance. Several other investigators have offered further elaborations on Bhutan's theory. In

2006, Med Jones, the president of the International Institute of Management, proposed tracking seven wellness areas: [5]

1. *Economic Wellness:* Indicated via direct survey and statistical measurement of economic metrics such as consumer debt, average income to consumer price index ratio, and income distribution

2. *Environmental Wellness:* Indicated via direct survey and statistical measurement of environmental metrics such as pollution, noise, and traffic

3. *Physical Wellness:* Indicated via statistical measurements of physical health metrics such as severe illnesses, being overweight, etc.

4. *Mental Wellness:* Indicated via direct survey and statistical measurement of mental health metrics such as usage of antidepressants and rise or decline of the number of psychotherapy patients

5. *Workplace Wellness:* Indicated via direct survey and statistical measurement of labor metrics such as jobless claims, job change, workplace complaints, and lawsuits

6. *Social Wellness:* Indicated via direct survey and statistical measurement of social metrics such as discrimination, safety, divorce rates, complaints of domestic conflicts, family lawsuits, public lawsuits, and crime rates

7. *Political Wellness:* Indicated via direct survey and statistical measurement of political metrics such as the quality of local democracy, individual freedom, and foreign conflicts

The most disappointing finding would be that as a nation's GDP increased, its happiness decreased. This could happen if people had to work longer hours, if both parents had to work, and if there was less time available for family and leisure.

At some point, many people realize they're in a "rat race" for higher income. They not only want to keep up with the Joneses, but even do better than them. They want a bigger home and a bigger car and further signs of success. They are kept going by envious comparisons with neighbors who do better and by the unceasing mass advertising power of huge companies that urge us to buy.

THE ROLE OF MATERIALISM IN RELATION TO HAPPINESS

Materialism is an orientation that is heavily promoted by economists and businesses. Materialism plays a major role in driving more consumer spending. We describe people as "materialistic" when they have a strong leaning toward acquiring and possessing material objects. We would not call a person "materialistic" who simply acquires basic food, clothing, and shelter. These are essential to living. However, if people spend a lot of time buying an unusual number of material objects, such as many dresses and pairs of shoes, we would label them as being materialistic. If they spend a lot of time searching and shopping for further goods even though their closets are full of everything they might need, we would say they have a materialistic addiction. If they are very conscious of their neighbors' possessions and want to acquire the same or even better possessions, they are materialistic.

The English poet William Wordsworth captured the spirit of materialism in his sonnet: "The world is too much with us; late and soon, / Getting and spending, we lay waste our powers; / Little we see in Nature that is ours; / We have given our hearts away, a sordid boon!"

The story is told of Abd Al-Rahman III, a wealthy emir in the tenth century who reigned for fifty years and who had everything in the way of material comforts, fame, and riches. He was asked how happy he had been. He answered that he could only remember fourteen days when he had pure and genuine happiness! Psychologists who have studied happiness and unhappiness point to the following conclusion: People who rate materialistic goals like wealth (and fame and sex) "as top personal priorities are significantly likelier to be more anxious, more depressed and more frequent drug users, and even to have more physical ailments than those who set their sights on more intrinsic values."[6]

Does this mean that materialistic consumers are typically unhappy? Not necessarily. A woman might wake up with the feeling that none of her wardrobe items fit anymore or are suitable for a forthcoming occasion, and she spends a whole day shopping for a new dress. She started out unhappy, got involved in the search without thinking about whether she was happy or unhappy, bought a nice dress, and is now happy, at least for a while.

We saw earlier that measuring happiness is complicated. A person's happiness can go up and down during the day. We need a measure of the more permanent state of a person's "well-being," "wellness," "contentment," or "life satisfaction." We can measure a whole population or subsample. It would be a good sign if a nation's reported level of "well-being," "contentment," or "life satisfaction" increased over time.

ACHIEVING HAPPINESS WITHOUT MATERIALISM

There are other styles of life than the materialistic that can give persons lifelong satisfaction. Among them are:

- Connecting deeply with art, culture, or religion
- Helping others and improving the world
- Deciding to live a simpler life with fewer possessions and needs

Let's examine these three paths to higher-purpose satisfaction.

Connecting Deeply with Art, Culture, or Religion

The world is a better place because, in every society, there are some people who have a deep feeling for art, culture, or religion. A few of them will be artists such as Michelangelo or Leonardo de Vinci who want to create beautiful or arresting pieces of art. There are architects who want to create impressive physical structures for living, governing, or worshiping. There are composers such as Beethoven, Mozart, or Verdi who stir our feelings with their beautiful musical compositions. There are religious leaders who inspire us to feel more spiritual about life and the world and its meaning. All of these dedicated people help build what we call a civilization and a culture.

Many creative people would not be able to thrive if it weren't for a much larger number of people who don't make art but who enjoy it and want to support it. Without patrons and purchasers, the artists would not have the financial means to pursue a life of art. The art lover is as important as the art maker. A culture suffers when fewer people in a society have the means or wish to support the art makers.

Helping Others and Improving the World

Among the most admired people are those who exhibit and extend caring behavior toward others, including strangers. We praise Mother Teresa, Mahatma Gandhi, and Nelson Mandela, who dedicated their lives to improving the lives of others. We admire persons who show prosocial behavior—that is, voluntary behavior intended to benefit others by donating, sharing, helping, cooperating, and volunteering. They are the people who respond to natural disasters by pitching in to save or help others. And in smaller ways, their high level of empathy leads to generous giving wherever a real need exists.

Prosocial behavior is central to the well-being of social groups. Encouraging prosocial behavior in children and young adolescents benefits society. Discouraging antisocial behavior also benefits society.

Some small measure of egotism or self-interest might operate in prosocial behavior. The giver receives a feeling of self-worth from doing a good deed. The giving or caring person may expect some reciprocity under certain circumstances. None of this diminishes the positive value added to the lives of the others who have received the caring and help.

Living a Simpler Life

Another nonmaterialistic path is to simplify one's life. Confucius said that a man would be admirable who lived in a mean, narrow street, with only a single bamboo dish to eat from, and did not allow his joy to be affected.

In Ancient Athens, the philosopher Epicurus held that the untroubled life is the source of happiness, and that the trouble of maintaining an extravagant lifestyle outweighs the pleasure of partaking in it.

There is a long history of famous people proposing a simpler life as the key to happiness. Among them are Gautama Buddha, John the Baptist, St. Francis of Assisi, Leo Tolstoy, Henry David Thoreau, Albert Schweitzer, and Mahatma Gandhi. Some religious groups, such as the Amish, Shakers, and Mennonites, have rejected pursuing wealth—or using technology.

One of the most influential thinkers on simplifying life was the economist E. F. Schumacher, who wrote *Small Is Beautiful* in 1973. Schumacher believed that the concentration of economists on output and technology was dehumanizing. He opposed the ideas that "bigness is better" and "growth is good." People were more important to him and nature was priceless. He advocated sustainable development and became a hero of the environmental movement. He questioned the appropriateness of using GDP to measure human well-being. He thought that the aim of people should be to obtain the maximum of well-being with the minimum of consumption. He used the phrase "less is more."

But seeking the simpler life is a direct attack on modern economics and modern marketing, which considers consumption and growth to be the sole end and purpose of economic activity. John Kenneth Galbraith saw the stockpiling of consumption goods to be the result of advertising and the "machinery for consumer-demand creation"[7] rather than based on actual need.

Those advocating simple living urge people to reduce consumption and to drop out of the high consumption game. They call for a radical shift from growth to "degrowth." By reducing consumption, people would reduce the time needed to earn money. They can then use this time for other interests, such as pursuing creative activities or helping others. By spending less, they can increase their savings, which can lead to financial independence and possibly earlier retirement. This type of thinking has spawned a number of "live simpler" movements:

- National Downshifting Week in the U.K. encourages people to live with less. The slogan: "Slow Down and Green Up."
- The 100 Thing Challenge is a grassroots movement to whittle down possessions to a mere 100 items, with the aim of decluttering and simplifying people's lives.
- The small house movement includes individuals who choose to live in small, mortgage-free, low-impact dwellings, such as log cabins or beach huts.

None of these campaigns have become mainstream movements. However, they do provide a platform for those who want to "drop out" from the "rat race." They also suggest a key way to deal with the challenge of growing unemployment.

Being Mindful of Consumption

I'd like to quote my good friend Jagdish Sheth, a professor at Emory University, on the impact of marketing on our lives. "Marketing has often been accused of promoting overconsumption, thereby compound-

ing the world's economic, environmental, and social sustainability challenges," he says. "There is widespread recognition of the need to adopt a
customer-centric sustainability approach and educate consumers while
also marketing products that avoid overconsumption and ease product
disposal. Traditional cultures typically practice the waste-not-want-not
philosophy, inculcated due to years of economic hardship. It is de ri-
gueur to sell old newspapers, bottles, and metal items to a trash vendor,
who then reuses or resells the items, for example, making paper bags out
of newspapers. As these societies adopt Western norms such local tradi-
tions may be forgotten and need to be reignited."[8]

HAPPINESS AND THE INEQUALITY OF INCOME

Although most people know about the exceedingly high incomes of famous movie stars, athletes, CEOs, and entrepreneurs, there doesn't seem
to be a mass outrage. The fact that the CEO of Boeing, James McNer-
ney, took home $27.5 million in 2013 was noticed by Boeing workers
only when the company insisted on cutting the pensions of its employees
rather than cutting the pay of top officials of the company. The fact that
a super-rich person can earn in an hour what an average person earns in
a year doesn't lead to any mass protest movements.

In China, there are about 500 protests a day calling for more wages
and/or better working conditions. It appears that in China, people are
less unhappy about the inequality of income than about whether they
have enough to live on. These people fail to see the connection between
wealth concentration and their not having enough to live on. Their biggest grievance is with corrupt officials who grab land, charge fines, and
demand bribes.

We don't hear much about income redistribution as a solution to
raising the incomes of average people. Most government legislators are
beholden to the rich to raise the money they need for getting elected or

reelected. Furthermore, they see the rich as driving the economy and conclude that breaking up concentrations of wealth would hurt investment in the economy or would cause the wealthy to flee from the economy. Little mention appears in the news media—also controlled by the rich—about the lavish incomes and expenditures of the super-rich. And there are always enough dreamers among the poor and working class who think that they too might get rich with a lottery ticket and live the life of Riley.

* * *

Redistribution has a role to play in maintaining a democratic society. The American and French revolutions were driven by the idea of creating a Society of Equals, where all citizens shared universal political and economic rights. It is a way to improve the participation of more citizens in the benefits of capitalism and democracy and to prevent the slide toward growing inequality that can lead to protests, crises, and further revolution instead of evolution.[9]

Here I summarize my thoughts about what is a feasible view about the constituents of a healthy capitalism:

- The aim of a capitalistic society should be to create an economic system whose operation leads to a broad level of happiness and well-being in its citizens.
- The task of a capitalist economy is to use its resources to permit all people to realize their potential and to obtain the basic necessities of life. The goal is to eliminate poverty.
- The job of marketing in a capitalist economy is to create a healthy desire in its citizens for the acquisition of material goods beyond the basics of food, clothing, and shelter. This might be called the American Dream.
- As a result of the public wishing to acquire more goods, people will work hard. Their jobs will produce a livable income that they

can spend freely to acquire the goods that they desire. And a responsible credit system allows them to acquire even more goods than they can afford with their current income within limits.

- As households earn an adequate income, their well-being increases. Beyond that level, a variety of factors will affect their level of happiness.

- Capitalism develops high-quality and luxury products to encourage its citizens to work hard to attain a "good life." The affluent middle class keeps the economy going.

- The hope is that the rich and super-rich take on more social responsibility to share their good fortune with those who are less fortunate.

EPILOGUE

Yesterday is gone. Tomorrow has not yet come. We have only today.
Let us begin.

— MOTHER TERESA

I wrote *Confronting Capitalism: Real Solutions for a Troubled Economic System* in order to better understand the role of capitalism in today's world economy. Capitalism is the chief mode of operation in most of the world's economies. It promises to lead to better economic performance, innovation, and value creation than any competing system such as communism or fascism. This is not to ignore its major shortcomings. I believe these shortcomings can be addressed with solutions that will improve people's lives.

The fourteen shortcomings are not independent of each other. They are highly interrelated. The problem of poverty is part of the problem of income inequality, which itself leads to low demand, which leads to too much unemployment, which leads to a clash between austerity and stimulus as two potential remedies, which is handicapped by political lobbying that gets legislators to vote for the causes that will keep them in power and therefore not vote for financial regulation and more environmental protection, and so on.

All this means that in working on any one problem, such as higher minimum wages, so many other issues come into play, such as some businesses possibly closing down, thus creating fewer jobs and more unemployment and incentivizing companies to import more goods from abroad, which leads to even less employment at home, and so on.

Legislators in a democracy tend to vote on one big issue at a time, neglecting these vast interconnections. Furthermore, they tend to prefer short-term solutions rather than to work on more difficult, long-term solutions. Failing to find long-term solutions is the cause of so many short-term problems.

Some people may throw up their arms in despair, given the odds of solving most of the shortcomings of capitalism. I am an optimist. I believe that there are enough intelligent, talented, and committed people who want to talk about these problems and hopefully create and agree on reasonable solutions. I mention solutions to each of these problems as a stimulus to thinking, knowing that a great amount of work must go into any final proposals. Hopefully, you the reader share my wish to improve the lives of people by helping capitalism work more effectively to bring about more material and spiritual well-being to the world's people.

NOTES

INTRODUCTION

1. "Survey Highlights a Troubling Divergence in the U.S. Economy. Message for Business Leaders and Policy Makers: A Coordinated Strategy Is Needed to Lift Living Standards for the Average American," Harvard Business School Press Release, September 8, 2014.
2. Hugo Dixon, "Britain Faces a Lose-Lose General Election," *New York Times*, September 29, 2014.
3. Palash Ghosh, "How Many People Did Joseph Stalin Kill?" *International Business Times*, March 5, 2013.
4. See Milton Friedman, *Capitalism and Freedom: Fortieth Anniversary Edition* (Chicago: University of Chicago Press, 2002) and Allan Meltzer, *Why Capitalism?* (New York: Oxford University Press, 2012).
5. See www.stwr.org/multinational-corps/key-facts.html. Also see Philip and Milton Kotler, *Winning Global Markets: How Businesses Invest and Prosper in the World's High-Growth Cities* (Hoboken, NJ: Wiley, 2015).
6. Bjorn Lomborg, ed., *How Much Have Global Problems Cost the World: A Scorecard from 1900 to 2050* (New York: Cambridge University Press, 2013).
7. Winston Churchill, House of Commons Speech, November 11, 1947.
8. Gar Alperovitz, "The Rise of the New Economy Movement," *Huffington Post*, July 12, 2014. Also see Alperovitz, *America Beyond Capitalism: Reclaiming Our Wealth, Our Liberty, and Our Democracy*, 2nd ed. (Takoma Park, MD: Democracy Collaborative Press, 2011).

CHAPTER 1: THE PERSISTENCE OF POVERTY

1. John Parker, "The 9 Billion-People Question," *Economist*, February 24, 2011.
2. Thomas Robert Malthus, *An Essay on the Principle of Population,* 1798.
3. Donella H. Meadows, Dennis L. Meadows, Jørgen Randers, and William W. Behrens III, *The Limits to Growth: A Report for the Club of Rome's Project on the Predicament of Mankind* (New York: Universe Books, 1972).
4. Paul Collier, *The Bottom Billion: Why the Poorest Countries Are Failing and What Can Be Done About It* (New York: Oxford University Press, 2007).

5. Jeffrey D. Sachs, *The End of Poverty: Economic Possibilities for Our Time* (New York: Penguin Press, 2005).

6. William Easterly, *The White Man's Burden: Why the West's Efforts to Aid the Rest Have Done So Much Ill and So Little Good* (Oxford, UK: Oxford University Press, 2006).

7. C. K. Prahalad, *The Fortune at the Bottom of the Pyramid: Eradicating Poverty Through Profits* (Upper Saddle River, NJ: Pearson Education, Inc. 2005).

8. Peter Edelman, *So Rich, So Poor: Why It's So Hard to Reduce Poverty in America* (New York: New Press, 2013).

9. "Census: U.S. Poverty Rate Spikes, Nearly 50 Million Americans Affected," CBS .com, November 15, 2012.

10. Tavis Smiley and Cornell West, *The Rich and the Rest of Us: A Poverty Manifesto* (New York, Smiley Press, 2012).

11. Edelman, *So Rich, So Poor.*

12. See Philip Kotler and Nancy R. Lee, *Up and Out of Poverty: The Social Marketing Solution: A Toolkit for Policy Makers, Entrepreneurs, NGOs, Companies, and Governments* (Upper Saddle River, NJ: Pearson Education, Wharton School Publishing, 2009).

CHAPTER 2: INCOME INEQUALITY ON THE RISE

1. Vilfredo Pareto (1848–1923) was an Italian sociologist, economist, and philosopher.

2. See http://givingpledge.org.

3. http://givingpledge.org.

4. http://patrioticmillionaires.org.

5. Thomas B. Edsall, op-ed on *Capital in the Twenty-First Century* by Tohmas Piketty, *New York Times,* January 28, 2014. http://www.nytimes.com/2014/01/29/opinion/capitalism-vs-democracy.html?nl=todaysheadlines&emc=edit_th_20140129&_r=0.

6. Edsall, "Capitalism vs. Democracy." Piketty says that the owners of capital absorbed a number of bad blows, including losing their credibility as markets crashed and losing physical assets in the two world wars. They were highly taxed to finance the two wars, suffered from high inflation that eroded the value of their assets, lost some major industries that were nationalized by England and France, and lost industries and properties that were appropriated in postcolonial countries. In addition, the trade union movement was strong under Franklin Roosevelt's New Deal and in the post–World War II period, enabling labor to participate in the economy's productivity gains.

7. Tyler Cowen, "Wealth Taxes: The Future Battleground," *New York Times,* July 21, 2013, p. 6.

8. Paul Vigna, "What's a CEO Really Worth? Too Many Companies Simply Don't Know," *Wall Street Journal,* November 21, 2014.

9. Ezra Klein, "10 Startling Facts About Global Wealth Inequality," *Washington Post,* January 22, 2014.

10. Annie Lowrey, "Even Among the Richest of the Rich, Fortunes Diverge," *New York Times,* February 11, 2014, p. F2.

11. See Paul Krugman, "Inequality, Dignity, and Freedom," *New York Times,* February 14, 2014, p. A25.

12. Christopher S. Rugaber, "Struggle Shows Up in Label," *Herald-Tribune,* April 3, 2014.

13. Jeffrey D. Sachs, *The End of Poverty: Economic Possibilities for Our Time* (New York: Penguin Press, 2005).

14. Tom Worstall, "Six Waltons Have More Wealth Than the Bottom 30% of Americans," *Forbes,* December 14, 2011. http://www.forbes.com/sites/timworstall/2011/12/14/six-waltons-have-more-wealth-than-the-bottom-30-of-americans/.

15. Gretchen Morgenson, "Invasion of the Supersalaries," *New York Times,* April 13, 2014, p. B1.

16. Larry Ellison of Oracle took home $96.2 million in 2011, but Oracle's board lowered his pay to $78.4 million in 2012. Ellison owns 25 percent of Oracle, and it is unusual for an owner to pay himself so much. His pay package rises or falls with Oracle's worth in the stock market and whether Oracle outperforms its competition. See Steven M. Davidoff, "Vote Against Executive Pay Rings Hollow," *New York Times*, November 7, 2013, p. 16.

17. Michael Dorff, *Indispensable and Other Myths: Why the CEO Pay Experiment Failed and How to Fix It* (Berkeley: University of California Press, 2014).

18. Jesse Westbrook, "Pay for Top-Earning U.S. Hedge Fund Managers Falls 35%," *Bloomberg*, March 30, 2012.

19. Paul Krugman, "Now That's Rich," *New York Times*, May 8, 2014.

20. Spencer Stuart Board Index 2013, pp. 33–34.

21. Morgenson, "Invasion of the Supersalaries."

22. Sam Polk, "Op-Ed: For the Love of Money," *New York Times*, January 19, 2014.

23. Annie Lowrey, "The Rich Get Richer Through the Recovery," *New York Times*, September 10, 2013.

24. Mark Gongloff, "Median Income Falls for 5th Year, Inequality at Record High," *Huffington Post*, September 17, 2013. http://www.huffingtonpost.com/2013/09/17/median-income-falls-inequality_n_3941514.html.

25. "Growing Apart," *Economist*, September 21, 2013, pp. 12–14.

26. Nicholas D. Kristof, "Why Let the Rich Hoard All the Toys?" *New York Times*, October 3, 2012.

27. "Inequality v Growth," *Economist*, March 1, 2014, p. 76.

28. Adam Withnall, "Pope Francis Tells Davos: 'Ensure Humanity Is Served by Wealth, Not Ruled by It.'" *The Independent*, January 22, 2014, p. 1.

29. See Philip Kotler and Nancy R. Lee, *Up and Out of Poverty* (Philadelphia: Wharton School Publishing, 2009), pp. 14–18.

30. Nafeez Ahmed, "Inclusive Capitalism Initiative Is Trojan Horse to Quell Coming Global Revolt," *Guardian*, May 28, 2014.

31. Dominic Barton, "Capitalism for the Long Term," *Harvard Business Review*, March 2011.

32. Ibid.

33. Joe Klein, "The Populist Mirage," *Time*, January 20, 2014.

34. Allan Sloan, "Positively Un-American Tax Dodges," *Fortune*, July 7, 2014, pp. 62–70.

35. See http://www.irishtimes.com/business/economy/us-wants-law-to-clamp-down-on-firms-moving-overseas-1.1867990.

36. Jacques Leslie, "A Piketty Protégé's Theory of Tax Havens," *New York Times*, June 15, 2014.

37. "Companies Keep Piling Up Cash Overseas," *Bloomberg BusinessWeek*, 2014, pp. 51–52.

38. "The Real Internal Revenue Scandal," *New York Times*, July 5, 2014, p. 10.

39. Eduardo Porter, "In New Tack, IMF Aims at Income Inequality," *New York Times*, April 9, 2014, p. B1.

40. Belinda Luscombe, "Do We Need $75,000 a Year to Be Happy?" *Time*, September 6, 2010.

41. Douglas K. Smith, "A New Way to Rein in Fat Cats," *New York Times*, February 3, 2014, p. A19.

42. "EU Proposes New Shareholder Powers over Executive Pay," BBC.com, April 9, 2014.

43. Kay Bell, "Tax Loopholes That Mainly Benefit the Rich." http://www.bankrate.com/finance/taxes/tax-loopholes-mainly-benefit-rich-1.aspx#ixzz2hpYhsMmV.

44. Chris Isidore, "Buffett Says He's Still Paying Lower Tax Rate than His Secretary," CNN Money, March 4, 2013.

45. "Carried interest," definition found at http://www.investopedia.com/terms/c/carriedinterest.asp.

46. Gretchen Morgenson, "When Taxes and Profit Are Oceans Apart," *New York Times,* July 5, 2014.

47. Ron Wyden, "We Must Stop Driving Businesses Out of the Country," *Wall Street Journal,* May 9, 2014.

48. Zaid Jilani, "How Unequal We Are: The Top 5 Facts You Should Know About the Wealthiest One Percent of Americans," *Think Progress,* October 3, 2011.

49. Fabian T. Pfeffer, Sheldon Danziger, and Robert F. Schoeni, "Wealth Levels, Wealth Inequality, and the Great Recession," Russell Sage Foundation, June 2014.

50. David Gilson, "Charts: How Much Have the Kochs Spent on the 2012 Election?" *Mother Jones,* November 5, 2012.

51. Stephen Gandel, "Buffett: Coke Exec Compensation Plan Was Excessive," *New York Times*, April 23, 2014.

52. Joe Nocera, "Buffett Punts on Pay," *New York Times*, April 25, 2014.

53. Stephen Gandel, "Buffett: Coke Exec Compensation Plan Was Excessive," *New York Times*, April 23, 2014.

54. James B. Stewart, "A Bonus Is Declined: A Problem Remains," *New York Times,* February 21, 2014.

55. Paul Krugman, "Paranoia of the Plutocrats," *New York Times,* January 27, 2014.

56. "Little Tax Haven on the Prairie," *BusinessWeek*, January 13–19, 2014, pp. 38–39.

57. See John Cassidy, "Forces of Divergence," *New Yorker,* March 31, 2014, pp. 69–73.

58. Peter Coy, "An Immodest Proposal," *Bloomberg BusinessWeek,* April 12, 2014, pp. 10–11.

59. Paul Krugman, "The Piketty Panic," *New York Times,* April 24, 2014.

CHAPTER 3: WORKERS UNDER SIEGE

1. Steven Greenhouse, "In Florida's Tomato Fields, a Penny Buys Progress," *New York Times*, April 24, 2014.

2. "Exploitative Labor Practices in the Global Palm Oil Industry," report prepared by Accenture for Humanity United, 2012.

3. Timothy Egan, "How to Kill the Minimum Wage Movement," *New York Times*, April 24, 2014.

4. Nancy DuVergne Smith, "MIT Living Wage Calculator: Why Higher Wages Help Everybody," *Slice of MIT* (blog), February 6, 2014.

5. Stanley F. Stasch, "The Creation and Destruction of the Great American Middle Class (1930–2010)," *School of Business Faculty Publications and Other Works.* Paper 5. http://ecommons.luc.edu/business_facpubs/5.

6. Sheila Bair, "Corporate America Needs to Raise Wages. Why? It's Good for Business," *Fortune,* July 21, 2014, p. 43.

7. Alan Pyke, "Republican Millionaire Has a Compelling Case for a $12 Minimum Wage, and He's Taking It Directly to California Voters," *Think Progress,* January 13, 2014.

8. Egan, "How to Kill the Minimum Wage Movement."

9. One of the most compelling cases against increasing the minimum wage is found in Gary Will, "Raise Minimum Wage? If ..." *Washington Post.*

10. "Poll Results, IGM Forum," *Igmchicago.org*, February 23, 2013, retrieved March 29, 2013.

11. Egan, "How to Kill the Minimum Wage Movement."

12. Paul Krugman, "Better Pay Now," *New York Times,* December 1, 2013.

13. Guy Standing, "About Time: Basic Income Security as a Right," in Guy Standing, *Promoting Income Security as a Right: Europe and North America,* 2nd ed. (London: Anthem Press, 2005), p. 18.

14. Annie Lowrey, "Switzerland's Proposal to Pay People for Being Alive," *New York Times Magazine*, November 17, 2013.

15. "New Research Findings on the Effects of the Earned Income Tax Credit," Center on Budget and Policy Priorities, retrieved June 30, 2010.

16. "Minimum Wages Only in Some Economic Branches in Germany," *Statistisches Bundesamt,* retrieved May 9, 2010.

17. Jonathan Cowan and Jim Kessler, "Capitalize Workers!" *New York Times,* April 6, 2014, p. SR 7.

18. Tony Hsieh, *Delivering Happiness: A Path to Profits, Passion, and Purpose* (New York: Business Plus, Hachette Book Group, 2010).

19. "Testing the Happiness Factor," The Drucker Institute, January 2, 2014.

20. Adam Davison, "A Ready-to-Assemble Business Plan," *It's the Economy,* January 5, 2014, pp. 12–13.

21. "Do Workplace Wellness Programs Save Employers Money?" Research Brief, Rand Health, 2014.

22. Shai Oster, "In China, 1,600 People Die Every Day from Working Too Hard," *Bloomberg BusinessWeek,* July 3, 2014.

23. Tanya Mohn, "U.S. the Only Advanced Economy That Does Not Require Employers to Provide Paid Vacation Time, Report Says," *Forbes,* August 13, 2013.

CHAPTER 4: JOB CREATION IN THE FACE OF GROWING AUTOMATION

1. http://www.pbs.org/newshour/rundown/more-than 200-million-people-were-unemployed-in-the-world-in-2013/.

2. Statement from Geoff S. Jones, Bennington, Vermont, *MIT Technology Review* 116, no. 5 (September–October 2013), p. 8.

3. Simon Head, *Mindless: Why Smarter Machines Are Making Dumber Humans* (New York: Basic Books, 2014).

4. See "The Emporium Strikes Back," *Economist,* July 13, 2013, pp. 23–25.

5. Jerry Mander, *The Capitalism Papers: Fatal Flaws of an Obsolete System* (Berkeley, CA: Counterpoint Press, 2012).

6. "Putting Released Prisoners Back to Work," *BusinessWeek,* February 6, 2014. In addition, in a *New York Times* editorial on May 24, 2014, titled "End Mass Incarceration Now," the main proposed solutions were summarized: "Reduce sentence lengths substantially. Provide more opportunities for rehabilitation inside prison. Remove the barriers that keep people from rejoining society after they are released from prison. Use alternatives to imprisonment for nonviolent offenders, drug addicts, and the mentally ill. Release elderly or ill prisoners, who are the least likely to re-offend…. Rate prisons on their success in keeping former inmates from returning."

7. Jeremy Rifkin, *The End of Work* (New York: Putnam Publishing, 1995).

8. See Erik Brynjolfsson and Andrew McAfee, *The Second Machine Age* (New York: W. W. Norton, 2014). Also see Tom Malone, *The Future of Work* (Boston: Harvard Business School Publishing, 2004).

9. "Briefing the Future of Jobs. The Oncoming Wave," *Economist,* January 18, 2014.

10. Robert J. Gordon, "Is U.S. Economic Growth Over? Faltering Innovation Confronts the Six Headwinds," NBER Working Paper #18315, August 2012.

11. This figure comes from "Game Plan for a Future-Ready Workforce," *Futurist,* November–December 2013, an interview with Ed Gordon, author of *Future Jobs: Solving the Unemployment and Skills Crisis,* conducted by Rick Docksai.

12. Philip Kotler, Hermawan Kartajaya, and David Young, *Attracting Investors: A Marketing Approach to Finding Funds for Your Business* (Hoboken, NJ: Wiley, 2004).

13. See Sean Higgins, "U.S. Ranks Below Rwanda, Belarus, and Azerbaijan in Ease of Creating New Businesses, World Bank Says," *Washington Examiner,* January 22, 2014. The rankings were included in the joint study undertaken by the World Bank and the

International Finance Corp., in *Doing Business 2014: Understanding Regulations for Small and Medium-Size Businesses* (Washington, DC: World Bank Group, 2013).

14. Jonathan Berr, "Billionaire Carlos Slim Argues for a 3-Day Work Week," *Money Watch,* July 2014.

CHAPTER 5: COMPANIES NOT COVERING THEIR "SOCIAL COSTS"

1. Dale W. Jorgenson, Richard J. Goettle, Mun S. Ho, and Peter J. Wilcoxen, *Double Dividend: Environmental Taxes and Fiscal Reform in the United States* (Cambridge, MA: MIT Press, 2013).

CHAPTER 6: ENVIRONMENT EXPLOITATION

1. Justin Gillis, "U.N. Panel Warns of Dire Effects from Lack of Action over Global Warming," *New York Times,* November 2, 2014, p. 1.
2. Paul Hawken, *The Ecology of Commerce: A Declaration of Sustainability*, rev. ed. (New York: HarperCollins, 2010).
3. Rachel Carson, *Silent Spring* (New York: Houghton Mifflin, 1962).
4. Donella H. Meadows, Dennis L. Meadows, Jørgen Randers, and William W. Behrens III, *The Limits to Growth: A Report for the Club of Rome's Project on the Predicament of Mankind* (New York: Universe Books, 1972).
5. "World Nuclear Association, Plans for New Reactors Worldwide," March 2013. http://www.world-nuclear.org/info/current-and-future-generation/plans-for-new-reactors-worldwide/.
6. Paul Vitello, "Ray Anderson, Businessman Turned Environmentalist, Dies at 77," *New York Times,* August 10, 2011.
7. Jacquelyn Smith, "The World's Most Sustainable Companies of 2014," *Forbes.com,* January 22, 2014. http://www.forbes.com/sites/jacquelynsmith/2014/01/22/the-worlds-most-sustainable-companies-of-2014/.
8. Peter Barnes, *Capitalism 3.0: A Guide to Reclaiming the Commons* (San Francisco: Berrett-Koehler Publishers, 2006).
9. Tim Jackson, *Prosperity Without Growth: Economics for a Finite Planet* (Abingdon, Oxon, UK: Earthscan, 2009).
10. Tim Jackson, "Prosperity Without Growth?" *Policy Innovations*, August 31, 2009.
11. Donella Meadows, Jørgen Randers, and Dennis Meadows, *The Limits to Growth: The 30-Year Update* (White River Junction, VT: Chelsea Green Publishing, 2004).
12. Jonathan Foley, Director, Institute on the Environment.
13. David Kashi, "Study Finds 37 Countries Face Severe Water Shortages: Study Suggests Water Shortages Affects Economy," *International Business Times,* December 13, 2013.
14. Daniel C. Esty and Andrew S. Winston, *Green to Gold: How Smart Companies Use Environmental Strategy to Innovate, Create Value, and Build Competitive Advantage* (New Haven, CT: Yale University Press, 2006).
15. Michael Grunwald, "The (Slow) Greening of America," *Time,* June 23, 2014.

CHAPTER 7: BUSINESS CYCLES AND ECONOMIC INSTABILITY

1. U.S. Business Cycle Dates, National Bureau of Economic Research, www.nber.org/cycles.html. The NBER sets the dates of troughs and peaks by making an informed judgment based on the course of various indicators such as real GDP, real personal income, employment, and sales.
2. See Kimberly Amadeo, "Business Cycle." http://useconomy.about.com/od/glossary/g/businesscycle.htm.

3. Charles Kindleberger, "Manias, Panics, and Crashes: A History of Financial Crisis."

4. Atif Mian and Amir Sufi, *House of Debt: How They (and You) Caused the Great Recession, and How We Can Prevent It from Happening Again* (Chicago: University of Chicago Press). Also see Peter Coy, "Sharing the Pain," *Bloomberg BusinessWeek*, pp. 12–13.

5. See Philip Kotler and John A. Caslione, *Chaotics: The Business of Managing and Marketing in the Age of Turbulence* (New York: AMACOM, 2009). Material in this chapter is drawn from this source.

6. Alan Greenspan, *The Age of Turbulence* (New York: Penguin Press, 2007).

7. "Business turbulence," *BNET Business Dictionary*. http://dictionary.bnet.com/index.php?d=turbulence.

8. Andy Grove, *Only the Paranoid Survive* (New York: Currency Doubleday, 1999).

9. Joseph Schumpeter, *Capitalism, Socialism and Democracy*, 3rd ed. (New York: Harper & Row, 1950).

10. Clayton M. Christensen, *The Innovator's Dilemma: When New Technologies Cause Great Firms to Fail* (Cambridge, MA: Harvard Business School Press, 1997); Clayton M. Christensen and Michael E. Raynor, *The Innovator's Solution: Creating and Sustaining Successful Growth* (Cambridge, MA: Harvard Business School Press, 1997).

11. "The Blood of Incumbents," *Economist*, October 28, 2004.

12. Harold L. Vogel, "Disruptive Technologies and Disruptive Thinking," *Michigan State Law Review*, no. 1, 2005. https://www.msu.edu/~michstlr/Symposium_2005/Vogel.pdf.

13. Fareed Zakaria, *The Post-American World and the Rise of the Rest* (London: Penguin Books, 2009).

14. See Nirmalya Kumar and Jan-Benedict E. M. Steenkamp, *Brand Breakout: How Emerging Market Brands Will Go Global* (Basingstoke, UK: Palgrave Macmillan, 2013).

15. "A Bigger World," *Economist*, September 18, 2008.

16. "Hypercompetition," *Wikipedia*. http://en.wikipedia.org/wiki/Hypercompetition.

17. Richard A. D'Aveni, *Hypercompetition: Managing the Dynamics of Strategic Maneuvering* (Glencoe, IL: Free Press, 2004).

18. D'Aveni, *Hypercompetition*.

19. "Sovereign wealth fund," *Wikipedia*. http://en.wikipedia.org/wiki/Sovereign_wealth_fund.

20. 2008 Sovereign Wealth Fund Institute Inc. http://www.swfinstitut.org/funds.php.

21. "A Bigger World," *Economist*.

22. "The End of Arrogance: America Loses Its Dominant Economic Role," *Spiegel Online*, September 30, 2008.

23. "Sovereign Funds Become Big Speculators," *Washington Post*, August 12, 2008.

24. "A Bigger World," *Economist*.

25. "From Risk to Opportunity," *McKinsey Quarterly*, October 2008.

26. "How Climate Change Could Affect Corporate Valuations," *McKinsey Quarterly*, October 2008.

27. Peter F. Drucker, *Managing in Turbulent Times* (Oxford, UK: Butterworth-Heinemann, 1981).

CHAPTER 8: THE DANGERS OF NARROW SELF-INTEREST

1. John Micklethwait and Adrian Wooldridge, "The State of the State," *Foreign Affairs*, July–August 2014.

2. R. Edward Freeman, *Strategic Management: A Stakeholder Approach* (Cambridge, UK: Cambridge University Press, 2010).

3. Philip Kotler and Nancy Lee, *Corporate Social Responsibility: Doing the Most Good for Your Company and Your Cause* (Hoboken, NJ: Wiley, 2005).

4. Philip Kotler, David Hessekiel, and Nancy Lee, *Good Works!: Marketing and Corporate Initiatives That Build a Better World ... and the Bottom Line* (Hoboken, NJ: Wiley, 2012).
5. Philip Kotler and Milton Kotler, *Market Your Way to Growth: Eight Ways to Win* (Hoboken, NJ: Wiley, 2013).
6. "Simon Anholt: Which country does the most good for the world?" YouTube video, 17:54, from TEDSalon Berlin, July 2, 2014.
7. Emily Ekins, "Reason-Rupe Poll Finds 24 Percent of Americans Are Economically Conservative and Socially Liberal, 28 Percent Liberal, 28 Percent Conservative, and 20 Percent Communitarian," *Reason Magazine,* August 29, 2011.

CHAPTER 9: THE DEBT BURDEN AND FINANCIAL REGULATION

1. Some of this section on the U.S. economy before the Great Recession follows the views of Richard Wolff in a number of talks he gave at various conferences that can be viewed on the Internet.
2. Arthur Laffer, quoted in Michael Bastasch, "Analysis: Real Stimulus Spending Is at Least $2.5 Trillion Since 2008," *Daily Caller,* August 6, 2012. http://dailycaller.com/2012/08/06/analysis-real-stimulus-spending-is-at-least-2-5-trillion-since-2008/.
3. Gallup Daily: U.S. Employment. http://www.gallup.com/poll/125639/gallup-daily-workforce.aspx36.
4. Interest Expense on the Debt Outstanding. http://www.treasurydirect.gov/govt/reports/ir/ir_expense.htm.
5. Jeanne Sahadi, "Washington's $5 Trillion Interest Bill," CNNMoney.com, March 12, 2012. http://money.cnn.com/2012/03/05/news/economy/national-debt-interest/index.htm.
6. "Budget sequestration," *Wikipedia.* http://en.wikipedia.org/wiki/Budget_sequestration_in_2013.
7. Mark Gongloff, "Median Income Falls for 5th Year, Inequality at Record High," *Huffington Post,* September 17, 2013. http://www.huffingtonpost.com/2013/09/17/median-income-falls-inequality_n_3941514.html.
8. http://www.globalpost.com/dispatch/news/afp/130918/fed-cuts-2013-2014-us-economic-growth-forecast-0.
9. "The U.S. Economy from 1970–2010, in 3 Charts." http://tipstrategies.com/blog/2011/08/a-tale-of-two-charts-employment-by-sector-1970-2010/.
10. "Income in the United States," *Wikipedia.* http://en.wikipedia.org/wiki/Income_in_the_United_States.
11. Tim Chen, "American Household Credit Card Debt Statistics: 2014." http://www.nerdwallet.com/blog/credit-card-data/average-credit-card-debt-household/.
12. "Household debt," *Wikipedia.* http://en.wikipedia.org/wiki/Household_debt.
13. Jessica Silver-Greenberg and Michael Corkery, "In a Subprime Bubble for Used Cars, Borrowers Pay Sky-High Rates," *New York Times,* July 19, 2014.
14. Editorial Board, "Payday Lenders Set the Debt Trap, *New York Times,* July 19, 2014.
15. Gary Hart, "The New Debate About Capitalism," *Blog,* January 12, 2012.
16. "Economy of the United States," *Wikipedia.* wikipedia.org/wiki/Economy_of_the_United_States#Finance.
17. Ralph Nader, *Unstoppable: The Emerging Left-Right Alliance to Dismantle the Corporate State* (New York: Nation Books, 2014).
18. Luigi Zingales, *A Capitalism for the People: Recapturing the Lost Genius of American Prosperity* (New York: Basic Books, 2012).
19. Robert J. Shiller, *The New Financial Order: Risk in the 21st Century* (Princeton, NJ: Princeton University Press, 2003).
20. Ibid.

21. Robert Creamer, "The Dominance of the Financial Sector Has Become a Mortal Danger to Our Economic Security," *Blog,* October 12, 2009.

22. Jesse Eisinger, "Soothing Words on 'Too Big to Fail,' but with Little Meaning," *The Trade,* December 11, 2013.

23. Zingales, *A Capitalism for the People.*

24. "Back from the Dead: The Return of Securitisation," *Economist,* January 11, 2014, pp. 59–60.

25. Adapted from Rana Foroohar, "The Myth of Financial Reform," *Time,* September 23, 2013, pp. 32–35.

26. Gretchen Morgenson, "Big Banks Still a Risk," *New York Times,* August 3, 2014.

27. Peter Eavis, "Wall St. Wins a Round in a Dodd-Frank Fight," *New York Times,* December 12, 2014.

28. Martin Wolf, *The Shifts and the Shocks: What We've Learned—and Have Still to Learn—from the Financial Crisis* (New York: Penguin, 2014).

29. *Economist,* May 31, 2014.

30. "A Better Model for Paying Bankers," *BusinessWeek,* October 23, 2014.

CHAPTER 10: HOW POLITICS SUBVERTS ECONOMICS

1. Gar Alperovitz, *America Beyond Capitalism* (Hoboken, NJ: John Wiley, 2005).

2. Francis Fukuyama, "The Decay of the American Political Institutions," *American Interest,* December 8, 2013.

3. Richard D. Wolff, "How the Rich Soaked the Rest of Us," *Guardian,* March 1, 2011. Also see Wolff's *Democracy at Work: A Cure for Capitalism* (Chicago: Haymarket Books, 2012).

4. Lawrence Lessig, *Republic, Lost: How Money Corrupts Congress—and a Plan to Stop It* (New York: Twelve/Hachette Book Group, 2011).

5. "Lobbying," *Wikipedia.* http://en.wikipedia.org/wiki/lobbying#cite_note-twsNovZ111-22.

6. http://en.wikipedia.org/wiki/lobbying#cite_note-23.

7. "Corruption Perceptions Index." http://cpi.transparency.org/cpi2012/#sthash.5W0Oh7Nn.dpuf.

8. John Kenneth Galbraith, *The Affluent Society* (New York: Houghton Mifflin, 1958).

CHAPTER 11: CAPITALISM'S SHORT-TERM ORIENTATION

1. Robert L. Reid, "The Infrastructure Crisis," *Civil Engineering—ASCE* 78, no. 1 (January 2008).

2. "New Infrastructure Survey Reveals U.S. Weakness and Need for Clear Vision," CG/LA Infrastructure LLC news release, October 4, 2011.

3. L. Randall Wray, "Developing the 'Financial Instability Hypothesis': More on Hyman Minsky's Approach," *EconoMonitor,* April 11, 2012.

4. Paul Davidson, "IKEA to Raise Its Minimum Wage," *USA Today,* June 26, 2014.

CHAPTER 12: QUESTIONABLE MARKETING OUTPUTS

1. See the excellent discussion in Robert and Edward Skidelsky, *How Much Is Enough?* (New York, Other Press, 2012).

2. Benjamin R. Barber, *Consumed: How Markets Corrupt Children, Infantilize Adults, and Swallow Citizens Whole* (New York: W. W. Norton, 2007).

3. "Economic Survey of the United States 2012," Organization for Economic Cooperation and Development, 2012. The Organization for Economic Cooperation and Development (OECD) is an international economic organization of thirty-four countries

founded in 1961 to stimulate economic progress and world trade. Its member countries are committed to democracy and the market economy.

4. "Why Is Health Spending in the United States So High?" OECD Health at a Glance 2011.
5. Richard H. Thaler and Cass R. Sunstein, *Nudge: Improving Decisions About Health, Wealth, and Happiness* (New York: Penguin Group, 2009).
6. Nancy R. Lee and Philip Kotler, *Social Marketing: Influencing Behaviors for Good,* 4th ed. (Thousand Oaks, CA: Sage, 2011).

CHAPTER 13: SETTING THE RIGHT GDP GROWTH RATE

1. http://www.worldofCEOs.com/dossiers/paul-polman.
2. Robert J. Gordon, "Is U.S. Economic Growth Over? Faltering Innovation Confronts the Six Headwinds," NBER Working Paper #18315, August 2012.
3. Donella H. Meadows, Dennis L. Meadows, Jørgen Randers, and William W. Behrens III, *The Limits to Growth: A Report for the Club of Rome's Project on the Predicament of Mankind* (New York: Universe Books, 1972).
4. Chandran Nair, *Consumptionomics: Asia's Role in Reshaping Capitalism and Saving the Planet* (Oxford, UK: Infinite Ideas Limited, 2011).
5. Herman Daly, *Steady-State Economics,* 2nd ed. (Washington, DC: Island Press, 1991), p. 17.

CHAPTER 14: CREATING HAPPINESS AS WELL AS GOODS

1. Richard Easterlin, "Does Economic Growth Improve the Human Lot?" Paper circulated at the University of Pennsylvania, 1971–1972 and published in 1974.
2. Thorsten Veblen, *The Theory of the Leisure Class* (New York: B. W. Huebsch, 1924).
3. John Kenneth Galbraith, *The Affluent Society* (New York: Houghton Mifflin, 1958).
4. Anne Muller and Tashi Wangchuk, *Gross National Happiness of Bhutan* (Jackson, WY: Pursue Balance, 2008).
5. Med Jones, "The American Pursuit of Unhappiness: Gross National Happiness (GNH)—A New Socioeconomic Policy," iim-edu.org, January 15, 2006, retrieved November 7, 2012.
6. See Arthur Brooks, "Love People, Not Pleasure," *New York Times,* July 18, 2014.
7. Galbraith, *The Affluent Society.*
8. Jagdish Sheth, personal correspondence with the author.
9. Pierre Rosanvallon, *The Society of Equals,* translated by Arthur Goldhammer (Cambridge, MA: Harvard Business Press, 2013).

INDEX

ABOUT THE AUTHOR

Philip Kotler is the S.C. Johnson & Son Distinguished Professor of International Marketing at the Kellogg School of Management, Northwestern University. At first he taught economics, but then Northwestern asked him to teach marketing and to bring more economics into it. Although now best known as a marketing guru, by passion and education, Kotler has always been an economist—having received both his M.A. and Ph.D. in economics and been trained by three Nobel economists. He received his master's from the University of Chicago, where he studied under the famed Nobel laureate and free-market evangelist Milton Friedman; he then pursued his Ph.D. in economics at the Massachusetts Institute of Technology (MIT) under the Nobel Prize-winning Keynesian economists Paul Samuelson and Robert Solow. Kotler then did post-doctoral work in mathematics and behavioral science at Harvard University and the University of Chicago, respectively.

As Kotler explains, the clear connection between marketing and economics is that marketing simply applies behavioral economics to understanding how consumers and producers make economic decisions in the marketplace. In marketing, he points out, we cover product innovation, pricing, channels of distribution, consumer economics, promotion, international trade, monopolistic competition, and many other areas of economics. In the emerging field of behavioral economics, essentially, Kotler is and has always been a behavioral economist.

Dr. Kotler has received honorary degrees from twenty-one foreign universities, and has consulted for countless companies, including General Electric, IBM, Merck, AT&T, Sony, Bank of America, Motorola, Ford, and many others. He has lectured extensively in India, China, Brazil, and Mexico, and in various other Asian, European, South American, and Middle Eastern countries. The *Financial Times* has included him in its list of Top 10 business thinkers.

He has authored more than 50 books, including his bestseller *Marketing Management*, which *Financial Times* cited as one of the 50 best business books of all time. Translated or adapted into more than 20 languages, it was the most widely adopted book around the world in MBA courses. Kotler's economics books include *Marketing Decision Making* (a treatise identifying the major factors that influence demand); *Marketing Your Way to Growth*; *Winning Global Markets*; *Up and Out of Poverty*; and now *Confronting Capitalism*.